KIDS IN CUFFS

KIDS IN CUFFS

Striving for Equity and
Empathy in Education

Ar'Sheill Monsanto

NEW DEGREE PRESS

COPYRIGHT © 2021 AR'SHEILL MONSANTO

All rights reserved.

KIDS IN CUFFS

Striving for Equity and Empathy in Education

ISBN

978-1-63730-654-3   *Paperback*

978-1-63730-737-3   *Kindle Ebook*

978-1-63730-928-5   *Digital Ebook*

To My Loving Tribe...

Thank you for holding me down during this process and keeping me grounded in the mission of the assignment.

This book is for you.

Kingston Monsanto, Kash Sinclair, Jeremiah Satterwhite, Noah Thigpen, Jason Davila, and Dylan Karter Harvey.

May you all grow to be strong educated men who change the world by spreading empathy and love, and being unapologetically YOU!

CONTENTS

———

*"Look closely at the present you are constructing:
It should look like the future you are dreaming."*

CHAPTER 1

MORALLY UNFIT AND GUILTY BY ASSOCIATION

———

It was summer 2019. I had recently passed my exam to receive my real estate license. I was waiting on my FBI background check to be completed so that I could get some sales while the market was still hot. HGTV had been my inspiration. I also loved the idea of helping people accomplish the goal of home ownership. Every day I would check the website in hopes of a response. I couldn't understand the reason for the delay. I had consented to many background checks for my profession and had never had an issue before.

After what seemed like an eternity, I finally received a response. It was not what I had expected. My entire body tensed up as I was informed that my license was on hold due to criminal activity that had shown up in my background. As I continued to peruse, I read that the real estate commission had deemed me morally unfit to practice as a sales agent. The background investigation had uncovered an arrest for an incident in high school. I had been sixteen years old at the time. This traumatic memory from twenty years ago was one I had deeply repressed. It was not an easy thing to forget, but I managed to put it behind me.

I was first heartbroken and confused, then humiliated. This was followed by embarrassment. How had a stupid mistake as a teen come back to haunt me as an adult? Beyond that moment, I had completed college and obtained a master's degree. I had a longstanding professional career in public policy, served on nonprofit boards, and mentored high school students. I was a doting mother to a handsome son, a loving wife, a homeowner, an entrepreneur, and a civically engaged taxpayer. I thought I had done everything right. But I was arrested as a youth for a situation that likely only needed intervention from a school counselor or mediator. It certainly had not warranted the interference of law enforcement.

One day during junior year, two students had been involved in a school fight. Fights were typically rare at our school but today was different. A friend of mine found out that the boy she dated also dated another girl at the school. Both girls were equally upset and by the end of the school day, an off-campus fight had ensued. As the two fought each other, each friend group watched the melee and was guilty by association. When we arrived on campus the next school day, we were forced out of our classrooms by school police officers. The officers handcuffed me and my friend together and escorted us to our lockers to gather our belongings. We were questioned about the incident and then automatically suspended. Then we were arrested in another wing of the school that served as a satellite police station.

It was not surprising that our school also housed a police station. The high school was located in the middle of Englewood, an extremely impoverished neighborhood on the Southside of Chicago. Before we entered the school grounds, we students sometimes faced daily bullying from the neighborhood kids. They would take the snacks we purchased from the corner store or the money we needed for lunch or bus fare back home. When we entered the school, we stepped through metal detectors. On the other side of the device, security officers searched our belongings and patted us down like an episode of *Law and Order: Criminal Intent*. As we traversed the halls to get to class, armed Chicago Police officers manned the halls looking for discretionary reasons to punish students. It was four years of trauma, coupled with standardized tests, fly-by-night friendships, and mediocre education at best. With this new suspension and arrest, I was now in tow to the school-to-prison pipeline.

The school-to-prison pipeline is the "practice of pushing students out of school and toward the juvenile and criminal justice system" (Flannery, 2015). Many factors contributed to this development, such as schools that have zero-tolerance discipline policies, mandatory suspensions, the presence of police at schools, and/or the lack of counselors and other resources for students. The school-to-prison pipeline was truly a phenomenon. For example, in 2010, three million students had been suspended from schools across the nation and 250,000 had been referred to law enforcement. For many students, the school-to-prison pipeline created sparse opportunities for education and limited economic opportunities. It was a trajectory to an overall bleak quality of life that infringed upon the rights to public education.

Within a matter of minutes, youth can go from being a student to being a criminal. Students make mistakes, and that lapse in judgment can come with automatic punishments. If students are considered special education and experience difficulties in their behavior or mood disorders, they are punished. Violation of the dress code—punished. Tardy or truant—punished. School discipline was a quick solution to a problem that had a deeper impact on policies, systems, and school environments.

When students experience exclusionary discipline in school they are often removed from their classroom and therefore are not learning. A study from the National Education Association indicated that the number of out-of-school suspensions in the 2015–2016 school year equated to over eleven million days of lost instruction. This loss was most common for Black boys and students with disabilities. Black and Latino students also accounted for 70 percent of police referrals (Flannery, 2015). There is no doubt that inequities existed. Yet there is a need for a new approach in order for education to be equitable for all students.

As a mother, I knew if the system continued to perpetuate itself as most systems do, there was a high likelihood my son could face similar circumstances when he became older. I decided to write this book to share the stories of people impacted by a system of oppression that often harshly punishes students or criminalizes trivial behavior. Oddly enough, these ineffective approaches to discipline filled the school-to-prison pipeline but did not change student behaviors. I want to provide you, the reader, with a better understanding of the current education system as well as potential solutions for change. This knowledge is foundational to creating new systems that exude empathy and equity and that work for all students.

DISCIPLINE SHOULD NOT REMOVE STUDENTS FROM LEARNING ENVIRONMENTS

I want this book to serve as a tool to radically disrupt current school discipline practices. Before we can tackle the behemoth of school discipline, we need to understand the roots as well as the offspring of the issue. For that reason, the first element of the book explores the area of school discipline through stories of students with firsthand experiences. In this section, I also examine the origin of police in schools, school codes of conduct, and their ramifications for students. My goal is for readers to notice the grim disproportionality that exists for students by subgroup. It's real and has a grave impact on academics.

The second element is more optimistic in that I share examples of school districts that are innovative. It begins with an analysis of what is happening with school discipline along with possibilities for change. I had the privilege of interviewing leaders that are doing things differently. Each person I interviewed in the book centered equity in their work. In 2020, masses of people demanded accountability from law enforcement, and that energy spilled into school board meetings. People questioned whether law enforcement and school districts should be in a relationship. Ultimately, I share some of the new policies that were written to be more anti-racist and equitable.

The last section of the book is the action element. I hope that readers understand the impact of policy, systems, and environments in schools. Discipline should not remove students from learning environments. Instead, we need to offer a more restorative approach to discipline. I want people to recognize that we decide what needs to change in our local schools. Every community is unique, but this framework is effective in shifting behaviors. Furthermore, you do not need to be a policy expert to change policies. You just need to be willing to dismantle systems!

SCHOOL DISCIPLINE STARTS EARLY

After working in the public policy/public health space for over fifteen years, I transitioned into a new role as Director of Strategy at an organization with a mission to eradicate inequity in schools. In doing research for my new role, I looked at videos about ending exclusionary discipline and the school-to-prison pipeline. Before this role, these terms were relatively new to my vocabulary, but I understood their definitions quite well. In high school, I had experienced firsthand many of the terms and practices I was formally learning about.

I discovered the negative way students of color are disciplined has been exacerbated as school policies have become stricter and the environments more hardened. A 2016 TEDx Talk video featuring a professor at the Metro State University named Dr. Rose Marie Allen explored the subject of early school discipline very well. In her talk, she postulated that school suspensions were quick solutions for adults but do not address the root of student behaviors. Immediately into the talk, she mentioned that in 2016 preschool students were suspended at "three times the rate of kindergarten through twelfth-grade students combined." I laughed because I figured it was a joke; it was not.

Dr. Allen continued to share that 40 percent of childcare centers and daycare centers in Illinois reported suspending children under the age of three. She went on to explain that Black kids composed 19 percent of the population of students in the early childcare setting but represented more than half of the suspensions. I could not wrap my mind around those statistics. Exclusionary school discipline started far earlier than I had originally thought. Much of the discipline was at the discretion of school leaders who believed children's behavior was somehow inappropriate and warranted punishment. It was subjective, latent with bias, and based only on the perspective of the decision-maker.

Watching the video reminded me of a time when I picked up my son from his private early learning academy. He was two years old. His small class had about ten children and few were Black students. It was a typical classroom filled with alphabets, blocks, and a colorful array of board books. On this day, the teacher informed me that my son had been reprimanded at her discretion for "throwing up signs" on the playground. I was immediately taken aback because from my perspective, only gang bangers threw up signs. She proceeded to show me pictures on her phone of my son and the hand gestures. At the age of two, he had the dexterity to manipulate his fingers to create a "peace sign" and "I love you" in American Sign Language. Even though my son was not suspended, it was clear to me the teacher did racially profile him.

As I continued to watch the video, Dr. Allen included information about her personal experiences of being suspended from schools. She noted that from her first journey to the classroom as a toddler through high school graduation, she was suspended about seven times per year. She provided insight on some of the reasons she was suspended which included digging a hole in the dirt on the playground. The reasons for her suspension seemed more aligned with child-like wonder and curiosity than deviant behavior. Yet research supports that: "Black students were more likely to be sent to the principal's office for subjective offenses like disrupting class" (Flannery, 2015). In Dr. Allen's case, one of her subjective offenses was playing in the dirt.

Another video I watched was gut wrenching. It depicted a young male with a scared expression on his face being arrested at school (When a School Calls the Police on a Student, 2020). I imagine he was not older than the age of twelve. He stood in a deserted school hallway replete with empty royal blue lockers that were half open. As the lone student in the hallway, he took orders from the police officer who was not in view of the camera. The student was ordered to raise his shirt, which exposed the tiny abdomen on his frail frame. He was then told to turn his body in the opposite direction so the officer could see his back. Still frightened, he complied with the commands.

His parents were not present. In fact, no teachers or other adults were there to protect the student. There was no one to make sure his rights weren't violated. The burly officer faced the camera and explained to the student that he was being arrested. He then proceeded to handcuff the student without reading him his rights. The arresting officer, Officer Moreno, made a dispatch call announcing that he was en route to book the student for a crime. In the vehicle, the officer shared with the student that once the school calls in police into any situation, the officer must follow law enforcement protocol. This could entail making an arrest. The student listened but looked like an afraid little boy longing for his parents.

When they arrived at the first intake facility the student being charged with the crime identified himself as Sammy Jordan. He was fingerprinted and photographed before being returned to the squad car. The officer then drove downtown to the larger juvenile justice intake facility. Jordan was told to face a wall. He was uncuffed, but only to walk through the metal detector. Another officer ordered him to remove his items, which included his shoes, striped shirt, and shorts. The student slowly undressed and handed the officer his clothing in exchange for a dark blue inmate uniform.

He was placed in a small cell where the officer closed the door and locked it. I could feel the loneliness and helplessness exuding from his facial expression. The final five seconds of the video displayed scrolling text that expressed gratitude for the police officers involved as well as the frightened student, who turned out to be only an actor. While this video was only a portrayal, the scenario was very real. No student should have to experience that.

EQUITY IN EDUCATION

Some people subscribe to the idea that students deserve to be punished for their behavior instead of determining the source of the problem. Black, Latino, and students with special needs often bear the brunt of antiquated racially biased school policies whether people admit it or not. These racially biased policies are perverse because the language is often vague. They are seemingly unobtrusive because the rules should in theory apply to everyone equally. These practices inadvertently give White students advantages that result in higher academic achievement and other opportunities while creating gaps for their counterparts. Moreover, these actions subconsciously uphold systems of oppression and are void of equity.

Due to inequitable discipline practices, students fall behind and are eventually pushed out of school. As an example, a 2018 United States Government Accountability Office report showed that Black students, males, and students with disabilities were more likely to be disciplined in schools. I was stunned to learn that Black students made up less than 16 percent of all enrolled students in public schools but accounted for 39 percent of the suspensions. Reading data like that especially concerned me as a mother of a Black son. Discipline practices such as zero-tolerance policies and stationing police in schools have evolved with little to no evaluation of their effectiveness. There is, however, evidence that shows a nexus between student outcomes and discipline (Connery, 2020). Fraught school discipline practices could be more restorative by providing equity and empathy.

There is an urgent need to create new practices that foster innovative mindsets. An example of innovation is restorative justice programs. Restorative approaches to school discipline have helped reduce both racial biases in how discipline is administered and diminish the use of exclusionary discipline as punishment. Restorative programs are derived from the teachings of indigenous people like the Navajo and Maori Native American tribes who used their principles as a way of life. It became popular in the United States in the 1970s (Gregory and Evans, 2020). Before its implementation in schools, it was widely used in the legal and justice system. It started its evolution into school settings with the intent of elevating mutual concern and respect for all members of the school system. Still, not all schools have bought into the idea of restorative justice. However, if properly implemented it can transform students and staff behaviors, which has a direct influence on school policies, procedures, culture, and climate.

Restorative justice is multifaceted in that it can help schools visualize preventative practices to address student misconduct, promote positive behavior, and foster accountability in students and staff. It can undergird alternatives to exclusionary discipline and enhance students' capacity for social-emotional learning. While specific elements of restorative justice can be implemented piecemeal, it is most effective as a comprehensive component of school culture. It's an innovative way to prioritize justice and equity, which traditional discipline approaches have lacked. This deficiency has led to present disparities in suspensions, expulsions, and arrests. However, based on a compilation of research, theory, advocacy, policy, and community organizing, it is possible to shift mindsets into a focus that accentuates equity in education.

CHAPTER 2

A BRIEF HISTORY OF RACIST POLICE POLICIES

———

HOW WE GOT HERE: A BRIEF HISTORY

The emergence of the relationship between law enforcement and public schools is multifaceted and was not designed in a vacuum. Shifts in policy, funding, and ideology perpetuated the growing relationship between education and law enforcement. However, the idea of uniformed police officers patrolling school hallways under the guise of school safety is rooted in the heart of the American Civil Rights Era. Therefore, the history of police in schools cannot be truthfully told without acknowledging its racist roots and the role law enforcement played that harmed students of color.

This historical framing of school police is important because it influences the modern-day school police. I wanted to learn more about school police because they seemed to be just as big a staple in the education system as teachers or books. I always questioned why they were there but never gave much thought to how they got there. Many questions swirled in my mind as I embarked on a quest for answers. The Texas State University's Texas School Safety Center asserts that the first law enforcement officer placed at a school as a school resource officer was in 1950 in Flint, Michigan, through the Police-School Liaison Program (2016). From the 1950s through the 1970s, America experienced a wave of civil unrest in the fight for equality throughout societal institutions. This sparked the Civil Rights Era. There was also resistance to inequality in education. The partnership between school resource officers and schools was to provide a proactive approach to fighting crime on school campuses (Texas School Safety Center, 2016). With that, police were brought into school buildings to protect White teachers and White students from students of color who often protested the disparities they faced.

Over the next decade, the emergence of school resource officers, which are "licensed peace officers employed by either the county or local law enforcement agency that are assigned permanently to serve the school district or campus," happened at a growing pace (Texas School Safety Center, 2016). Concurrently, by 1960, schools began to employ their own law enforcement departments. Laws had changed and predominantly White schools were now required to integrate with other races. There was pushback, and local police were brought in to protect White students and White teachers from students of color who entered their schools. Five years later, Congress passed the Law Enforcement Assistance Act to "provide grant dollars for the training of law enforcement to strengthen crime control" (1965). Minneapolis and Tucson were among the first two cities to receive this federal funding in the amounts of $70,000 and $60,000, respectively (Zhang, 2020). By 1970, one percent of all schools had some form of law enforcement on campus (Connery, 2020). Today over half of all schools in the nation have a police presence.

Slightly different from the original school resource officer model, the advent of school districts having their own police force started in Boston. The 1950s school resource officers model utilized sworn officers assigned to a specific school long term. As I pored over my research, I stumbled upon a podcast that addressed the historical context of school police. I put on my headphones and took copious notes, fascinated by their evolution and my own ignorance in tandem. According to the podcast "Have You Heard," in Boston during the 1960s, Black residents protested government housing segregation, a lack of sanitation services, and police brutality (2020). In 1963, the NAACP education committee accused the Boston school committee of operating and maintaining segregated schools. This demand for basic human dignity was largely ignored. It ignited more protests as Black students, parents, and civil rights leaders began to organize boycotts at schools.

By 1968, another wave of Black student activist emerged with even bigger demands. They advocated for the hiring of more Black teachers and counselors, as well as changes to the school's code of conduct and discipline policies. They also wanted a curriculum that was more relevant and culturally conscious. These demands were immediately met with much opposition and caused Black students and their families to be outraged, which resulted in more protest. A judge eventually ordered Boston schools to create a new safety and security department to protect the school. This birthed a pseudo-police force for Boston Public Schools (Berkshire and Schneider, 2020). That organization still guards Boston Public Schools to this day, despite its insidious past.

PUSH BACK AGAINST A SYSTEM

The hosts continued to elaborate on the disorder and inequality students of color were experiencing. "What's helpful with the Boston story and thinking about this during segregation, that also happens in other cities throughout the country, is that you see the establishment of police in schools is directly connected to racist ideas of criminality" (Berkshire and Schneider, 2020). The hosts suggested that the ramifications of students protesting for equal treatment later become an access point for "the expansion of prisons, police and American life."

Essentially the host described the concept of the school-to-prison pipeline burgeoning in the 1960s. This was way before the term was coined. Policies that uplift the school-to-prison pipeline firstly encourage the presence of police in schools by contracting with local police forces or creating a districtwide police department (Chiariello, et al. 2013). Officers are empowered to use force or physical restraint, often by handcuffing students who misbehave, especially when no policy prohibits it. Most importantly, police have the authority to arrest students on and off campus for nonviolent offenses. Other school practices that foster the school-to-prison pipeline include exclusionary discipline that removes students from their classrooms during learning times instead of positive behavior interventions. Nebulous language like "a disruption" was grounds for suspension. Students who protested injustice were considered disruptive. This increased the likelihood that students would encounter police, get arrested, and eventually be incarcerated.

In the 1960s, more and more students began to protest the inequity in schools. In 1968, fifteen thousand students, teachers, and activists walked out of seven different schools in East Los Angeles in protest of educational inequity. At the time, the high school dropout rate for Latino students was 60 percent. The students who successfully graduated high school on average read at an eighth-grade level compared to their White counterparts (Berkshire and Schneider, 2020). On the "Have You Heard" podcast, guest Matt Krauz, a doctoral student at Teachers College, Columbia University said, "What we can see here is students pushing back against a system that was really designed for White students and controlled by White adults." Furthermore, local governmental entities upheld and reinforced these blatantly unfair, insidious practices.

The protestors formed the Educational Issues Coordinating Committee because Latino students were infuriated with the school district and the lack of resources for equal access. For example, Latino students were banned from speaking Spanish in school, their native language. They were not provided many options to seek college opportunities but instead were guided toward vocations (Contreras, 2011). Their demands included a dual-language curriculum, smaller class sizes, and the hiring of teachers who were reflective of the student body. The Los Angeles Unified School District did not take steps toward remediation with the organizers citing a lack of funding as the reason it could not be done. Instead, the sheriffs were called into the situation. When the sheriffs arrived, they donned riot gear and forced the students to return to class to receive their subpar education. The students rebelled! In the process, thirteen organizers were arrested on felony charges and potentially faced a life sentence in prison for conspiracy to disturb schools. Eventually, everyone was released without serving jail time (Contreras, 2011). While the demands of the school district were not immediately met, community organizing was a powerful tool for causing changes in the system. In 2020, history repeated itself as Los Angeles school district students mobilized to remove police from schools.

After over a decade of passing landmark education policy via *Brown vs. the Board of Education,* students of color still experienced grave disparities in schools. *Brown vs. the Board of Education* called for equal treatment under the law, but that was not the case. In contrast, their White counterparts have faced a vastly different understanding of the education system. Law enforcement worked on their behalf to uphold illegal segregation and other unequal treatment of non-White students. Students of color, on the other hand, experienced cruelty. When school districts decided to involve law enforcement, it enhanced the idea that police were necessary to curtail the violence caused by students of color. It made it seem like law enforcement was an essential response to resolve the situation and make schools more secure for White students. In the process, police in schools have alienated students and made them feel less safe (Advancement Project, 2016).

TOUGH ON CRIME

I continued to listen to the "Have You Heard" podcast as the host shared data that felt closer to home for me. I knew what had caused the emergence of police in other cities, but what about Chicago Public Schools? That was where I had my first encounter with the police as a teen. I learned the Chicago Teachers Union advocated for more police on campus to protect teachers over fifty years ago (Berkshire and Schneider, 2020). The Chicago Teachers Union used the criminal case of a special education student, Lee Hester, as the reason why more police were needed in school. Hester was a Black, fifth-grade student who was fourteen years old at the time and several grade levels behind. In 1961, Hester had allegedly murdered a forty-five-year-old White elementary school teacher named Josephine Keane inside of their school.

The student was named as a suspect because a teacher merely suggested he could be guilty of the violent murder. This was a baseless claim. Hester was then arrested and questioned by police. He did not have representation of a lawyer nor was a parent present. The cognitively challenged student confessed to the murder although physical evidence had contradicted his confession. The jury found him guilty of the crime and fourteen-year-old Hester was tried as an adult. Modern studies show that students with learning disabilities, despite making up less than 10 percent of the school population, account for 32 percent of students in juvenile detention centers (Chiariello, et, al. 2013). Research for the aforementioned study was conducted decades after Hester's case but shows that this practice has deep roots.

Hester's case was appealed multiple times even at the Supreme Court level, but the conviction remained. One final time in 2014, the case was reinvestigated. Five years later, Lee Hester, a man well over the age of seventy, was finally exonerated of the crime he did not commit. It was believed that a White janitor with mental health issues employed by the school had murdered Ms. Keane. He had also confessed this to a psychologist (Possely, 2020). Many students today who are Black and/or have a disability are likely to have a similar experience with the school-to-prison pipeline as Hester. Tragically, Hester spent a huge portion of his life incarcerated for a crime he did not commit.

HARDENING CHICAGO PUBLIC SCHOOLS

The formal creation of police in Chicago Public Schools happened in 1966. The Chicago Police Department had a contract to hire off-duty police officers to provide security for Chicago Public Schools. Principals of the schools requested those off-duty officers patrolling schools to wear their full uniform, which included their badge and service weapon. During that first year, the force consisted of six officers, but by 1972 the police force was about five hundred officers (Kunichoff, 2017). Over time, the number of police staff continued to grow.

In 1991, Chicago Mayor Richard Daly required two police officers on all high school campuses in the Chicago Public School system as gang violence grew in neighborhoods. This was part of his tough-on-crime stance that bubbled during the 1990s (Kunichoff, 2017). The problems associated with violence happened throughout the community. However, instead of undertaking societal issues by creating jobs or providing social services, funds were used to harden schools. Metal detectors and police substations were placed inside of high schools to process students that have been arrested on campus (Kunichoff, 2017). This aligned with my memory of my Chicago Public High School experience. Police and security guards were present at almost every nook and cranny of the school building.

Fast forward five decades and the Chicago Teachers Union shifted its stance and advocated in support of the removal of police in schools. In June 2020, the union released a statement expressing their disdain for the Chicago mayor and school board. They voted in support of a $33 million contract with the Chicago Police Department (D'Onofrio et al., 2020). This was despite most school buildings being physically closed and many students attending school online. A month later, the Chicago Teachers Union Research Department published an online report with the position that police do not make students or staff safer (Counselors Not Cops: Research Behind the Call for Police-Free Schools, 2020). Their research indicated that the presence of police often criminalized student behavior. Police unnecessarily created an undue pathway where students were arrested by police, then referred to court, and eventually incarcerated.

The report from the Chicago Teachers Union purported that police in schools simply increased stress levels and contributed to the school-to-prison pipeline. It boldly called to defund police budgets. In contrast, the union recommended reallocating those funds to hire more counselors, nurses, social workers, and psychiatrists. These additional personnel would be better equipped to address the needs of students who are "ill, distressed, or traumatized." Schools that invested in these services for students experienced an increase in attendance rates, higher academic achievement, and increased graduation rates along with decreases in disciplinary actions, reductions in suspensions, and declines in expulsions.

POLICE DO NOT PREVENT SCHOOL SHOOTINGS

As a parent, there is nothing more devastating than the thought of a school shooting. Schools should be safe places that foster learning. In terms of police in schools, very little research shows that police in schools prevent school shootings. Police were not initially brought into schools to counter school shootings. The initial purpose of school police was to uphold systems of segregation that fundamentally marginalized Black students and other students of color. The creation of police in schools occurred long before that phenomenon. However, a surge in police presence in schools peaked in the 1990s.

There is very little data to assess whether the presence of police in schools deter violence or stop school shootings (James and McCallion, 2013). A 2018 study by the *Washington Post* reinforced this idea by analyzing school shooting data that occurred after the shooting at Columbine High School (Cox and Rich, 2018). The Columbine High School shooting sadly claimed the lives of thirteen people and injured dozens of others. After that, the presence of police in schools increased (Ahmed and Walker, 2018). School shootings, although mortifying, are still considered extremely rare. In early 2018, school shootings claimed the lives of seventeen students and teachers in Parkland, Florida. In that same year, a fifteen-year-old student murdered sixteen people in a high school in Benton, Kentucky. Ten people were also killed in a high school in Santa Fe, Texas, also during that year. Aside from shootings that happen in school buildings, other incidents occurred where students were harmed by a gun adjacent to a school, like in its parking lot.

In the analysis, the *Washington Post* also discovered that sixty-eight schools with police officers or school security personnel had experienced gun violence. Yet in most cases, the shooting ended before law enforcement or security could intervene. Police arrived after the tragedy had happened, unfortunately. There was only one incident of a school shooting where a school police officer was able to take down an active shooter in the nearly 200 schools they used for their research (Cox and Rich, 2018). A congressional report reaffirmed this ideology. "Research suggests the presence of an SRO might result in more children being involved in the criminal justice system for minor offenses, and this, in turn, can result in other negative consequences, such as higher rates of suspensions or greater likelihood of dropping out of school" (James and McCallion, 2013). For schools that predominantly serve students of color, the harm outweighs the good.

Lastly, in 2021, the American Civil Liberties Union in Washington published an online report. The report cited a study conducted by the FBI and Texas State University that investigated over one hundred incidents on campus, including twenty-five school shootings. The results were that shootings in school typically ended in one of two ways: either the gunman was apprehended by unarmed staff like a teacher, or the shooter decided to stop firing. Multiple reports show that school resource officers do not play a vital role in these situations. Moreover, school-based law enforcement departments historically have received tons of grant dollars without oversight. There is very little data collection on the effectiveness of school police. On the other hand, the same report pointed out that a vast majority of schools do not meet recommended ratios for counselors, licensed social workers, nurses, and psychiatrists. This is a problem with a simple solution.

RADICAL REFORMS FOR EQUITY

Radical reforms that reimagine the role of police in schools are essential for students to truly receive an equitable education. We must be mindful that the inception of law enforcement in schools derived from the desire to arrest students who protested an inequitable education. In 2020, University of Louisville Assistant Professor Ben Fisher shared research findings that indicated school resource officers placed in affluent schools with a predominantly White student body viewed their role as keeping students safe (Samuels, Christina A, 2020). On the other hand, police officers placed in urban schools with predominantly Black and Latino populations saw the students as threats. It is inherently harmful to employ school resource officers or contract with local law enforcement officers who possess this mindset patrolling school hallways. It questions the idea of what is considered "safety" and who is being "protected." As a student, I never felt safe with the police on campus.

This relationship is problematic for students because school districts disperse millions of dollars toward law enforcement by employing thousands of school resource officers or contracting with local police departments. Often, the funding earmarked for law enforcement is not proportionate with funding allocated for mental health resources. Some arguments point out that school resource officers are believed to follow a triad model where the role assignments include "enforcing the law, counseling students and teaching staff and students about safety issues (Texas School Safety Center, 2016). Yet there is very little research indicating students seek school police for counseling or have built positive relationships.

Besides, students should have access to professional staff on campuses like mental health counselors and psychiatrists. They can help students navigate situations and get to the root cause of problems. Many school resource officers are not trained in trauma-informed care and lack certifications in counseling. Only trained and licensed counselors should provide counseling services to students, just as only certified educators are allowed to teach. Police officers should not fill gaps in school staff or administer discipline to students.

There is also a need for consistency and continuity in protocols for school discipline and the role of law enforcement. Standard practices in policing tend to vary by district and sometimes even vary by campus within the same district. School resource officers and police deployed to campuses should be specifically trained and experienced in interacting with youth. Schools with large populations of students of color should also require unconscious bias training for officers so students of color are not over-policed as research suggests they have been. Moreover, teachers and school administrators should be equipped and trained to handle misconduct as part of their classroom management.

CHAPTER 3

KIDS IN CUFFS

TOY GUNS ARE TOYS FOR KIDS

One Friday, I picked up my son from preschool as I did on most weekdays. Before gathering his belongings, I spent a few moments talking with his teacher about his day. She gave him a glowing review and showed me artwork he had created with finger paint. The following Monday, the COVID-19 virus struck Houston and the rest of the world. The entire city abruptly shut down, and that included school buildings.

My son never returned to his school or had the opportunity to say a proper farewell to his classmates or teachers. For over a year, my son and I stayed home, only going to the outside world for essential trips like grocery shopping. Since many of our normal sources of entertainment had come to a halt, we spent a lot of time being creative. I would often glance over at my son to find him coloring scribbles on pieces of paper. One of these days he walked up to me with a drawing and announced he had made a portrait of me. It was an abstract doodle but if I squinted hard and shifted the paper a tiny bit to the right, I could see the resemblance. Obviously, it was not a perfect image but all the components of a face were there. It just required a bit of imagination and an open mind to what it could be. It made me realize that now was the time to reimagine our education system to be fair and equitable for all.

I doomscrolled national online news headlines about the turmoil of education during the COVID-19 pandemic. As people struggled to learn about the coronavirus and its ramifications, inequities in the education system were front and center. Grief and anxiety were high, and still, Black male students were facing additional hurdles to accessing their education due to school discipline in the form of virtual suspensions (Edmonds, 2020). Suspensions prior to the COVID-19 pandemic were typically high for Black students, but now students were being removed from virtual classrooms for a myriad of reasons.

There were stories in my newsfeed about Black male students suspended during virtual learning for having toy guns within view during online instruction. I came across a story about a twelve-year-old Black student at Grand Mountain School in Colorado Springs who experienced a virtual suspension (Peiser, 2020). Virtual suspensions, similar to suspensions from school buildings, removed students from class and denied them learning opportunities. According to the article, this boy, Isaiah Elliot, was suspended for five days on the claim that he brought an object indistinguishable from a firearm to "school" despite being in his home. The teacher who instructed the class remotely called law enforcement into the situation.

The student's mother, Danielle Elliot, recounted how the assistant principal informed her that law enforcement was on their way to her residence because of the toy gun. Mrs. Elliot attempted to resolve the misunderstanding before it became an issue by emailing the teacher to explain it was just a toy (Peiser, 2020). I continued to read the article between interactions with my son about his doodle. I noticed my table, which now served as a desk, was peppered with notepads, large pencils with the foam grips, Post-It notes, my son's crayons, LEGO blocks, and his favorite Nerf guns and darts. These Nerf guns were not a threat or an endangerment to safety. They were simply toys for children.

I didn't understand why an adult teacher would assume a bright green toy was an actual firearm. But a study from the American Psychology Association, indicated that starting at age ten, Black boys are seen as less innocent than their White peers (Goff, et, al., 2014). If teachers expect bad behavior from specific students, they look for it and then punish them for it. Stereotypes and unconscious bias are huge contributors to this type of behavior. This heinous treatment of Black students stemmed from structural racism and created gaps in opportunities.

Similar to Elliot, in Louisiana, a fourth-grade student, Ka'Mauri Harrison, was also suspended for having a toy gun in view during online instruction time (Crespo, 2020). The *CNN* news article reported that the student was taking a test when a sibling, with whom he shared a room, walked in and tripped over the toy BB gun lying on the floor. Harrison moved the toy gun from the floor to a place near his desk and continued to take his test, thus putting it in view during class time. The article went on to describe that the teacher attempted to get the student's attention but was unsuccessful because the sound on his computer was muted during testing.

At some point, the student lost connectivity because of his internet. From there, the teacher then reached out to his parents and grandparents to explain the student had a "gun" in class, the "class" being his shared bedroom. For the infraction, the school district initially recommended that Harrison be expelled from school. Later, the district amended the punishment to a six-day suspension and a social work assessment (Crespo, 2020). A simple misunderstanding made a lasting impact on Harrison and the state of Louisiana. It reinforced how widespread institutional racism is in schools and how it perpetuates unequal educational opportunities when students are removed from class. School policies needed to be updated, especially in the age of virtual learning.

The American Civil Liberties Union of Louisiana released a statement about the suspension stating "Ka'Mauri Harrison's suspension from school was an excessive and unjustified punishment that reflects the deeply rooted racism that criminalizes Black students and fuels the school-to-prison pipeline" (Odoms, 2020). The Executive Director of the ACLU also cited a statistic from Tulane University's Education Research Alliance for New Orleans that Black students are twice as likely to be suspended than their White peers. That report examined discipline data across Louisiana and noticed disparities in discipline across the same school district (Barrett, et, al., 2017). This meant that campuses within the same school district were not aligned on specific parameters for how to address student behavior. Punishment was subjective and based solely on the ideals of the person administering the discipline.

Harrison's family filed a lawsuit against the school district seeking damages. They requested the student be allowed to make up missed instruction time due to the suspension according to a local news article (Burke, 2020). Months later, the school board reduced the suspension from the original six days to three (Roberts, 2020). Nevertheless, the student had already served the six-day suspension months prior. During the fall special legislative session, the Louisiana State Legislature adopted House Bill 80 named the "Ka'Mauri Harrison Act," which required school systems to adopt new discipline policies for virtual learning (Romero, 2020). In addition, the law provided processes for students to make appeals to punitive decisions like the named virtual suspensions. The legislation also made the policy retroactive to March 2020, the onset of the global COVID-19 pandemic.

School rules established eons ago were being adopted and adapted to a virtual learning setting with little discretion or understanding of other issues at play. School and home life were now meshed together with little to no boundaries. Reading these news articles was infuriating as a parent. I cringed seeing students who looked like the slightly older version of my son being punished for arbitrary interpretations of the school code of conduct. Despite the confusion in the world brought on by the pandemic, I was not completely surprised by what was happening. Research affirmed that Black students are more likely to be punished in schools than White students for the same offense and are generally seen as problematic students (Riddle and Sinclair, 2019). The school-to-prison pipeline was still in full operation. Even in the virtual setting, Black students were still criminalized. The difference now was that law enforcement was making house calls instead of arresting students in the halls of a school. When learning in their own homes, students should not be accused of bringing "weapons on campus," especially if it is a toy gun.

Discipline practices that remove students from class put them at academic risk. This practice lacks equity and has disproportionate consequences on students of color and those with disabilities. The Center for Public Education asserts that equity is achieved when schools are properly funded, students receive rigorous instruction, and teachers are highly qualified (Barth, 2016). Qualified teachers should be well versed in their subjects and other topics that aid in their professional development like training to address unconscious bias.

The National Education Association EdJustice suggests that training around bias can examine "structural oppression or racism and assess how organizational structures, practices or governing documents" affect interactions with students. When teachers are equipped to understand unconscious bias, it can lead to better engagement with students. SRI's Education Center for Learning and Development also concluded that it could help educators better understand themselves by self-reflecting on their own perspectives and experiences. Fundamentally, training in unconscious bias has the potential to shrink the discipline gap and promote equity and justice for students (2021).

USE OF FORCE

During a seemingly normal day, a seventeen-year-old Cedar Creek High School student named Noe Niño de Rivera ended his school day by being airlifted to a hospital in a medically induced coma (McLaughlin, 2014).

In a school district near Austin, Texas, at a campus called Cedar Creek High School, a fight ensued between two girls in a hallway. De Rivera was among the students in the crowd witnessing the altercation. One of the students happened to be his high school girlfriend, according to statements from his attorney (McLaughlin, 2014). The local county sheriff's department contracted with the school district to serve as school resource officers and Deputy Randy McMillian arrived at the fight scene. De Rivera was attempting to break up the fight when officers arrived on the scene (McLaughlin, 2014). This good Samaritan action turned out to be a big mistake for De Rivera.

While school fights are not uncommon among adolescents, they should never result in bodily harm to students at the hands of police officers. Still, Deputy Randy McMillan, invoking his right as a peace officer, decided to use a taser on De Rivera. Data shows that school police officers increasingly use force techniques like tasing students to stop misbehavior, according to a Texas Appleseed report (School Police, 2016). The report indicated school district police departments often provide officers with items like pepper spray, tasers, batons, and canines despite the danger these tactics pose to students' young bodies. Moreover, Black and Hispanic students were disproportionately represented in the use-of-force incidents at school.

Many school districts allow the use of force on students irrespective of unclear guidance on utilization (School Police, 2016). Officers are allowed to lean on their discretion for usage. According to an *Austin-American Statesman* news article, when De Rivera was tased by the officer, he collapsed to the concrete floor and hit his head on the way down (O'Rourke, 2018). In an article on De Rivera's attorney's website, the attorney indicated that the taser company provided a disclaimer that their equipment should not be used on any minors (Loewy, 2014). The jolt left De Rivera nearly lifeless and suffering from a brain hemorrhage. Unfortunately, no medical aid was rendered while the student was handcuffed nearly unconscious.

De Rivera was taken to the county hospital but was later airlifted to St. David's Medical Center in Austin (O'Rourke, 2018). His injuries were so extreme he was put into a medically induced coma where he remained for over fifty days. He missed nearly two months of his life and weeks of academic instruction. After regaining consciousness, De Rivera did not return to his normal life. He spent time in recovery at an in-patient brain injury rehabilitation program. The amount of trauma the student, his family, and his classmates experienced is unimaginable. There is an opportunity to replace these extreme policies with alternatives that do not increase the risk of death and injury for students.

The National Association of School Resource Officers produced a report titled *The SRO & Prevention of Violence in Schools* to address criticism of school safety policies and the role school resource officers play on campus. This publication was among the body of research the association regularly disseminated to its members for best practices. Throughout the report, it stated that strong school resource officer programs "effectively protect and serve the school community." It further noted that officers were duty-bound to keep students safe from harm. Most importantly, an officer's role in school discipline should be defined in a Memorandum of Understanding between the local law enforcement agency and the school district. This means that school leaders and law enforcement should work together to establish criteria for school offenses as well as protocols for use of force.

In the case of De Rivera, he was neither involved in the fight nor carrying any weapons. Witnesses and camera footage shown on *CNN*'s website provided evidence of this. As a best practice, school resource officers who observe violations of the school code of conduct should escort the students to school administrators. School discipline should then be determined solely by school administrators (Canady, et.al., 2012). This seems reasonable and the safest option for students. If Deputy McMillan felt that De Rivera was breaking a rule by trying to end the fight, he should have taken the student to the principal's office. In spite of it all, De Rivera suffered unnecessary violence at the hands of school police (McLaughlin, 2014). The practice of state sanctioned violence is dangerous for students. School leaders need to work collaboratively to figure out ways to address student behavior more humanely so incidences like this do not happen again.

The charges against Deputy Randy McMillan were dismissed, and he was never held accountable for hospitalizing De Rivera. Legal documents reported in the *CNN* article stated, "The actions of Deputy McMillan were the actions of a reasonable officer" because the student failed to comply with the police officer's orders. The officer was apparently justified in tasing the student who he should have been protecting. De Rivera's attorney was successful in gaining a semblance of restitution in settling the case for $775,000, which helped cover medical and rehabilitation expenses (Loewy, 2014). But the student's life was forever changed.

The fact remains that De Rivera was neither the first nor the last student to be tased by school-based law enforcement. In fact, he is lucky to be alive as Texas ranks third in the nation for deaths associated with tasers (School Police, 2016). Until policies change students remain at risk of being victimized by the adults who should be keeping them safe. No kid should end up in handcuffs for minor offenses on campus. This can be circumvented by banning the use of force on students and further determining the role that school police should play in school discipline. No student should have to endure abuse like that of the violence inflicted upon De Rivera.

STRIVING FOR EMPATHY

"Empathy is the key to encouraging prosocial behavior, limiting aggression, and diminishing social prejudice in our world" (Amico, 2020). This definition posits that current education systems would be different by placing a value on how we assess student achievement. It also mentioned that "educating children in, and with, empathy also has a direct effect on their behavior and motivation." It listed other scholarly studies that draw connections between the effects that empathy has on students and higher academic achievement. Most importantly, the article suggested that empathy is a skill that can be learned and that I believe is more restorative than traditional punishment typically used in schools.

I first met Jess Coles when we were randomly paired together in a Zoom breakout room through our Civic Voices in

Education Fellowship cohort. The fellowship focused on how to address systemic inequities in education by engaging community leaders, educators, and administrators. In our initial conversation, we discussed racial equity in public education. We shared our career backgrounds with each other and what we hoped to gain from the nine-month learning experience. Coles mentioned she was a former educator and served at an organization that promotes equity and accountability in public schools. I was intrigued. After our brief conversation, our Zoom breakout room closed, and we were back with the full group of fellows.

Weeks later, we virtually crossed paths again when she joined a community organizing workshop a coworker and I facilitated. The workshop touched on the basic skills required to shift power dynamics for systems change. It required people to listen with intention as well as search deep within themselves to figure out what agitated them enough to want to disrupt systems. We asked our participants to reimagine school systems in which equity and empathy were front and center, since public education has been less than fair for many students of color throughout US history.

In the workshop, we addressed at length the 1946 *Silvia Mendez v. Westminster* Supreme Court case of the nine-year-old student who sued a California school district because of segregation. Civil rights attorney Thurgood Marshall was part of this case's legal team and used this ruling as precedence for the more widely known case of *Brown v. The Board of Education*. Our conversation pivoted to how modern-day school codes of conduct policies were as harmful to Blacks and students of color as Jim Crow laws were in the past. For instance, many schools remain segregated, and schools that predominantly serve students of color typically lack resources and are overpoliced.

Months later, I reached out to Coles and asked if she would be willing to tell her story for the book. I wanted to know how her experience with school discipline had impacted her life. She began by sharing her experience in high school. The first high school she had attended was a small, rigorous magnet school of about five hundred high-performing students. In the interview, she lovingly described the school's culture as tight knit because everyone knew each other. She mentioned there were rarely any discipline issues with students she could remember.

The next school year, her family moved across town, and she was no longer in the same school district. Her new school was starkly different in that there were roughly five thousand students on campus. She remembered being "extremely overwhelmed" on the first day by the large sum of people. Despite the school's large population, she mentioned feeling somewhat lonely in the new environment. In her opinion, she also felt the school's environment was more aggressive as she witnessed students being combative toward each other. This often resulted in students getting suspended.

She vividly recalled a time when police officers entered her classroom and ordered the students to leave so the canine units could search their belongings for illegal drugs. She insinuated it was normal for students to feel like criminals and it was just another facet of the school's culture at the time. While the presence of school police was mentioned multiple times throughout our conversation, she never spoke of intervention mechanisms like school counselors. Research from the American School Counselor Association suggested that counselors have specialized skills in preventing the disruptive behavior of students (2019). If these resources were adequately available, it could have helped create a more positive learning environment for students.

I was fascinated by her story because many of the details she shared felt familiar. In our conversation, she mentioned a day when she arrived at school and was frantically approached by several students. The students informed her that another student at the school did not particularly like her and wanted to fight her. During the school year, she had less-than-friendly interactions with this student on many occasions. However, she still wanted to amicably speak with her directly because they had mutual friends. During the lunch period when the two spoke, the other student became aggressive and violently pushed Coles. Like anyone, she defended herself against the student and a fight quickly happened in the cafeteria. It was the first and only fight she ever had, but it made a lasting impact.

For starters, both students were detained by school police officers, but only Coles received an in-school suspension referral. An in-school suspension is a form of discipline where students are suspended from their normal academic schedule and must report to a specific room on campus that is not the student's normally assigned classroom (Policy Areas, 2013). The school had a zero-tolerance discipline policy and was not interested in hearing details that led up to the incident. A fight automatically resulted in suspension even if a student felt she was being bullied, which Coles suggested throughout the interview. Coles shared that she never had a chance to tell her side of the story. The administrators did not look at her stellar academic record or her extreme engagement in many extracurricular activities that made her a well-rounded student. From my understanding, the entire situation lacked equity and empathy. The school enforced the policy without assessing the individual student and her needs, and it definitely did not embody values to repair harm.

In 2019, the American School Counselor Association posited that disruptive student behavior is a serious, ongoing problem in most schools. Research implies disruptive behavior is common and impacts students in the classroom. This can have an influence on the school's environment as well. A remedy is for school districts to invest in mental health staff and other resources for students. The association also recommended creating school discipline policies with input from school counselors. While counselors should help create policies, they should not be involved in administering discipline. School administrators like principals and deans should handle discipline. Counselors instead should maintain relationships with students and serve as mediators or student advocates. It is imperative that counselors take on these duties and not school police officers. If Coles' high school had similar practices in place, her situation could have had a different outcome.

In our interview, she shared, "From that moment, I was just, like, in this system, and it was this bureaucratic process of how to deal with me. It was like a one size fits all." She thought it was excessive because in addition to the suspension, she told me she "was on probation for about a year. I had to take anger management classes and character-building classes." Anger management is a therapeutic approach that should have been a resource available to students on campus instead of being ordered by the juvenile court system. She was also required to do community service. After fulfilling those requirements, she was able to move forward with her academic career despite almost trekking a pathway into the school-to-prison pipeline.

After graduating from college, she returned to the classroom, this time as a math teacher. Her high school experience empowered her to view education and how students are treated through an empathy lens. As we wrapped up our conversation, she talked about a former student who had a disability that prohibited him from being punctual. The school was aware of that diagnosis. One day, the student was absent from Coles' class because another teacher had written him a referral for in-school suspension due to his constant tardiness. Coles retrieved the student from the in-school suspension room because it was unfair to punish him for being tardy because of his disability. The referring teacher did not have a relationship with the student and was unaware of his needs.

Empathy can start with relationship building. Coles emphasized she felt building relationships promoted a more welcoming environment for students and made her a more effective teacher. She lamented that she would have wanted more empathy from educators when she had her incident with discipline in high school. Coles was almost a victim to the school-to-prison-pipeline because of zero-tolerance discipline policies at her school. While she was successful in avoiding the downward spiral, until schools make changes to how discipline works in school, many students are still at risk of that phenomenon.

CHAPTER 4

CONSEQUENTIAL CODES OF CONDUCT

RELYING TOO HEAVILY ON SCHOOL POLICE

School codes of conduct are rules and expectations communicated to students and parents outlining expectations of behavior as well as consequences associated with violations of the said code. Overall, school codes of conduct are necessary to create a safe environment for students (Codes of Conduct Policies). These policies, in theory, apply to all enrolled students equally. However, data and anecdotal research show that school codes of conduct have created less-than-equitable school environments. Some codes of conduct possess vague language that overly punishes students of color by suspension or expulsion.

One of the most egregious examples is in the 2015–2016 school year, during which Black boys made up 8 percent of enrolled students but accounted for 25 percent of out-of-school suspensions (DeVos and Marcus, 2016). In comparison, White male students comprised 25 percent of enrollment and proportionally represented 24 percent of suspensions. Also, school codes of conduct rely heavily on school police in response to disciplinary actions that would not be considered a crime outside of a school.

During the 2014 school year, sophomore high schooler Ixel Perez was violently arrested at school by three officers. The student was detained by school police for checking text messages in class, according to an article in the *Huffington Post* (Lohr, 2017). As it goes, the student was in her reading class when she checked a message on her phone from her father about the whereabouts of her disabled mother. Her mother's disability included only having 15 percent of her kidney and needing constant dialysis treatment. Her father had reached out to her in the middle of the school day because he was unsure where his ailing wife was at the time.

The school code of conduct banned the usage of cell phones by students during instruction time (Student Requirements/ Code of Conduct). For that reason, Perez's teacher immediately asked her to relinquish the phone because it violated the school code of conduct. The exigent circumstances did not matter. After the student did not do as requested, the assistant principal intervened by also demanding the cell phone. Still, Perez continued to refuse the request and walked away from the assistant principal. The assistant principal then decided to bring law enforcement into a disciplinary issue of student misconduct (Lohr, 2017). It's possible that after Perez responded to the messages and ascertained her mother was safe that she possibly would have stopped using the phone. But the situation continued to evolve because school leaders often rely heavily on school police to handle trivial matters around student behavior (School Police, 2016).

At the time of the incident, Perez weighed one hundred pounds and stood under five feet tall. In a *Huffington Post* article, Perez is quoted as saying, "One of them was behind me, like on my legs and trying to put the handcuffs on." While being restrained the small teen was slammed to the ground by three police officers. "It hurt a lot and the other cop had his knee on my head, all his weight on me, and I was screaming because it hurt so much" (Lohr, 2017). This dangerous restraint tactic has caused death to some people who were subdued in that manner. Some police forces have even banned its usage (Ian, 1993).

Perez, although defiant, did not commit a crime by checking text messages in class. It was a violation of the rules with seemingly clear consequences. When students use cellphones in class, teachers confiscate them until students pay a fee for their return (Student Requirements/Code of Conduct). The school code of conduct considers it a Level 3 Act of Misconduct when a student refuses to give a cell phone to staff. At this level of misconduct, students either receive a parent/teacher conference, exclusion from extracurricular activities, in-school suspension, up to three days for out-of-school suspension, or "other disciplinary responses" as a consequence. The latter ambiguous language is harmful to students because the punishment is then left to the discretion of the staff. Refusing the request can include a combination of all the aforementioned consequences. It can also embody something more serious like the involvement of law enforcement as a means of "other disciplinary responses."

Codes of conduct should serve as guides on how administrators should respond to situations that require discipline. The role of law enforcement should be clearly defined and should not include restraining students over a cell phone. While data from the US Department of Education suggested the restraint of students was fairly infrequent, Hispanic students make up 17 percent of restraints. This is based on national data from the 2015–2016 school year where 124,500 were physically or mechanically restrained. The number is small in comparison to the entire population of students in school, but it is significant to the thousands of students that directly experienced similar use of force by school police. The data does not disclose reasons why police used force so it can encompass grave offenses like a student attacking another student with a weapon or very small matters like using a cell phone in class. Furthermore, school police should be trained to deescalate situations that are non-criminal offenses.

POLICING BLACK HAIR

Racial bias plays a significant role in school discipline and there is an urgent need to dismantle antiquated policies rooted in racial discrimination. Princeton University researchers reviewed the role of racial bias in school discipline. Their research drew on data from thirty-two million elementary through high school students who received disciplinary action (Riddle and Sinclair, 2019). Their findings showed that Black students were four times more likely to be punished than any other subgroup. Similarly, an article from Brookings reported that 70 percent of suspensions of Black students were for discretionary offenses like violation of hair policies in the school code of conduct (Henderson and Bourgeois, 2021). Students were being punished because of hair.

In January 2020, high school senior De'Andre Arnold, along with his younger cousin, Kaden Bradford, a junior at the school, were suspended for wearing locs as a hairstyle. In 2019, the school district's policy required that boys' hair not extend below the eyebrow, ear lobes, or the top of a T-shirt collar (Barbers Hill ISD Student Handbook: 2019–2020 School Year). The school deemed that both students' hairstyles violated the school's code of conduct's dress code (Grieder, 2020). Before the hair incident, both boys were outstanding, well-rounded students who participated in extracurricular activities and sports. Ultimately, their academic records were tarnished because of misconduct associated with wearing a hairstyle relevant to their family's culture. The district denied their policy on hair was racially motivated. In an *ABC13 Houston* news article the district's superintendent, Greg Poole stance was, "Our policy limits the length. It's been that way for thirty years." Be that as it may, many perspectives and policies have changed since the 1990s to be more inclusive.

While the policy did not prohibit braids or locs as long as they met the aforementioned lengths, it was still latent with bias. The locs were a salient part of both students' cultural identities. There was also language that explicitly mentioned that hair should not be "distracting" and should be "appropriate." This type of language is a breeding ground for discretionary suspensions. In Texas, 88 percent of all disciplinary actions in 2018–2019 were for discretionary violations to the school code of conduct (Ensuring Safe and Supportive School Climates in Texas, 2020). Moreover, Black students comprised 13 percent of the student body in Texas but accounted for 32 percent of suspensions and 20 percent of expulsions. Hairstyles were among some of those violations. The cousins, Bradford and

Arnold, chose not to disavow their heritage by cutting their hair to assimilate into the school's culture.

As a result, both students were suspended from school along with other consequences. Arnold was not allowed to participate in his senior graduation ceremony, and when Bradford returned, he was sentenced to in-school suspension for the remaining school year. The punishment was extremely harsh, but research showed that Black students in Texas were five times more likely to be suspended than their White peers (Ensuring Safe and Supportive School Climates in Texas, 2020). Because of this discrimination, the two student families decided to file a lawsuit against the school district. They argued the students had been intentionally racially discriminated against under the protection of the Fourteenth Amendment's equal protection clause and Title VI of the Civil Rights Act of 1964 (LDF Files Public Records Request on Behalf of De'Andre Arnold and Family, 2020).

The students were denied an education due to suspension because of a hairstyle. A federal judge ruled the dress code policy was discriminatory and prevented the school district from enforcing the policy (Justin, 2020). With the stroke of a pen, Bradford was able to return to school without fear of in-school suspension while the lawsuit was ongoing. His cousin Arnold, being a senior when the incident began, had already graduated from high school. However, at the close of the school year, the *Houston Chronicle* reported that school board trustees unanimously voted to keep the discriminatory dress code policy in place (Gowdy, 2020). The following school year, the *Houston Chronicle* reported that the same school district had referred over thirty students to in-school suspension for violations of the very same policy (Dellinger, 2021).

The incident of Arnold and Bradford, along with a myriad of others that did not make headlines, inspired members of the Texas Legislative Black Caucus to draft its own version of the CROWN Act. The legislation is an acronym for Create a Respectful and Open World for Natural Hair Act (The CROWN Research Study, 2019). The act was birthed from a research study on hair discrimination designed "to ensure protection against discrimination based on race-based hairstyles by extending statutory protections to hair texture and styles such as locs in the workplace and public schools." The Texas bill would have prohibited discrimination in student dress codes or a school's grooming policy (Bowers, 2021). It had the propensity to impact thousands of Black students like De'Andre Arnold and Kaden Bradford. However, despite having an outpouring of support for the legislative bill, the Texas CROWN Act did not pass.

Students should not have to worry about their hair being a reason for punishment. When my son arrived in the world, he donned a head full of lavish, black curls. Whenever we would take a stroll to the park or a baby Gymboree class, strangers could not resist the urge to touch his hair. I found this to be inappropriate. As he got older, his curly coiffeur became part of his signature style. When my son turned four, he asked for locs like his father and older cousin. My husband and his nephew wore locs because of their cultural heritage of being of Belizean descent. My husband has grown locs for over a decade and the length extended beyond his waist at the time. In our household, locs are a source of pride.

There is an opportunity for school districts across the nation to reexamine policies that have marginalized students. In

2031, my son will enter his freshman year of high school. I am more than certain that by then he will have transformed his head full of curls into long locs like his father. I want him to embrace his cultural identity without jeopardizing his access to education. When also reviewing outdated policies, schools should also focus on professional development around cultural competency, diversity, equity, and inclusion. Most importantly, school systems need to stop vilifying students by policing their natural hair and hairstyles.

BLACKS GIRLS AND SUBJECTIVE DISCIPLINE

Proponents of school dress codes argue that it fosters equality because all students are bound to the same rules. Before school buildings closed their doors due to the COVID-19 pandemic, I volunteered with a nonprofit organization that partnered with schools to provide a life skills curriculum to young ladies. The high school where we served consistently failed to meet state standards and accountability ratings for several years (Jacob, 2019). Many of the young women who were part of our sessions often ran the gamut of discipline issues and our nonprofit provided a much-needed positive outlet.

We often started our sessions by sharing roses and thorns that had happened to us during that week. During these conversations, the young ladies would share something good that happened as their rose and something less positive as their thorn. Too often, the girls would mention a discipline referral by a teacher as their thorn. Those who chose to elaborate mostly mentioned a violation of the school uniform policy or willful defiance, which constituted speaking to a teacher in a way deemed disrespectful or disruptive. It seemed superficial, but I heard the same claims week after week. The girls were constantly in trouble and spent tremendous amounts of time missing class because of suspensions for these frivolous matters. These discipline measures were exacerbating the achievement gap at a school where many of the students were already not meeting standards and had long fallen behind.

Black girls were at a disadvantage in terms of receiving an equitable education by virtue of their race. A study in 2017, reviewed school discipline records and interactions between students based on race and gender. The research showed that Black girls were three times more likely to receive a discipline referral than their White counterparts. Those infractions were for issues like "disruptive behavior, dress code violations, disobedience, and aggressive behavior" (Morris and Perry, 2017). They weren't too different from what I heard in our sessions in the school where I volunteered. The aforementioned punishments were very subjective and had a disproportionate impact on Black girls like the young ladies we served in our nonprofit program. Morris and Perry's research suggested the complexity of why Black girls were overly disciplined involved unconscious bias and stereotypes that teachers may use to judge students' behavior. Interpretations of Black girl behavior, in whether students were disobedient or the like, were based on the opinion of school officials.

Another research report showed the disparity in how Black girls were often punished compared to girls of other races due specifically to dress codes. In 2018, the National Women's Law

Center commissioned a study titled "Dress Coded: Black Girls, Bodies, and Bias in DC Schools" (Brodsky, 2020). This small study looked at twenty-one Black girls from twelve schools enrolled or recently enrolled in the DC public school system. The purpose of the study was to investigate problems with dress codes and policies on grooming, their racial implications, their impact on academic achievement, as well as how they are enforced.

The most overwhelming statistic from the report was that Black girls were an astonishing twenty times more likely to be suspended from DC public schools than White girls (Brodsky, 2020). The main reason was for violations of the school dress code, which had very specific guidelines on what can be worn by girls. Even if the intentions of a school dress code were altruistic, all students were not experiencing the policy as such. When students were noncompliant, which might mean they wore a tank top or leggings, they were made to leave their classroom to go home and change. In doing so, these girls are not in their classroom learning.

A reason why Black girls were often overly corrected for minor behavior is that they were seen as less innocent and more adult-like than White girls their same age. A report from Georgetown Law Center on Poverty and Inequality asserted this age compression starts as early as age five and continues through age fourteen. Through this viewpoint, adults placed expectations on Black girls that characterized them as developmentally older. They are thought to need less nurturing and protection (Epstein, et, al., 2017). Stereotypes also played a role. This makes behavior like being an outspoken girl who advocates for herself seem more like willful defiance. Because these young girls appear as adults, they are seen as more culpable for their behavior and often punished accordingly. This malpractice contributes to the overrepresentation of Black girls who are disciplined. This subjectivity does not only happen on campus; it also occurs in the juvenile justice system.

In the juvenile courts, on average, a mere three out of ten court cases that involved Black girls were dismissed at the discretion of the prosecutor. Conversely, seven out of ten cases involving White girls were dismissed (Epstein, et al., 2017). For example, in 2020, a fifteen-year-old Black girl was incarcerated for not doing her schoolwork, according to an article in *Pro Publica*. In the past, the girl had been arrested for assault and theft but was beginning to atone for her wrongdoings. Completing her schoolwork was a condition of her probation (Cohen, 2020). Like many schools across the nation, at the onset of the COVID-19 pandemic, schools took their instruction online. This transition was not easy for all students.

The student had ADHD along with an Individualized Education Plan. When she did not receive the additional support outlined in her IEP, she struggled to focus during virtual learning. The student eventually stopped logging on. Since the student's probation was contingent upon academic performance that she did not complete, the judge revoked her probation at the request of the student's caseworker (Cohen, 2020). She was handcuffed and sent to a juvenile justice facility. It was an extremely harsh sentence for simply not completing schoolwork.

REDUCE RACISM AND INCREASE EQUITY

Codes of conduct can adversely impact students, especially when the guidelines are obscure and obsolete. A doctoral candidate at the Neag School, Britney Jones, suggested a framework that reduces racism and increases equity in school policies. Her framework was developed from research of twenty-five schools across the world that had equity and/ or anti-racism policies and/or practices in place. The exemplar policies from her research assured that school districts understood the importance of equity along with a plan to mitigate racism. This is important when revising codes of conduct because research shows that students of color are punished at far greater rates than their White counterparts (King and Lhamon, 2015). In schools, the focus should be on education and not removing students from their lessons when they exhibit deviant behavior.

According to Jones' research, school leaders need to build awareness of racism and equity before they can create policies to correct these issues. In doing so, school leaders can have mindful conversations about the effects of systemic and even individual acts of racism. This entails examining policies, systems, and environments in schools that may perpetuate the oppression of students (2020). Providing equitable educational opportunities for students takes willingness from school leaders to do the work. Leaders should prioritize equity by recruiting and retaining staff who are dedicated to anti-racism. This approach should be paired with professional development opportunities that train on unconscious bias and cultural competence. Another element that is vital for equity, according to Jones' analysis, is to review data and make the appropriate change if there is overrepresentation of particular groups. Lastly, Jones identified funding as a critical component to support and sustain equitable change. These small shifts can promote inclusive school environments and policies that are free of cultural or gender bias.

For starters, to reduce racism and increase equity, school districts should unequivocally adopt anti-racism policies. Similar to school codes of conduct, anti-racism policies can serve as guiding principles that show the districts' commitment to dismantling racism along with the protocols followed to reach this goal (Jones, 2020). In her research she found that schools that were effectively eradicating racism had written policies adopted by their board of trustees. This helped frame the issue of racism and provided an understanding of the issue as it related to the operation of the school district. Sound policies relied on a combination of research, data, and input from stakeholders like students, parents, teachers and staff. Anti-racism policies often run side by side with an equity statement that identifies key priorities previously discarded by the anti-racism policy (Jones, 2020). As an example, if a school district's anti-racism statement addressed an end to punitive discipline policies, the equity policy should outline alternative programs like the implementation of restorative justice programs. Lastly, the policies needed to be communicated from the superintendent and trickled down all the way to students as part of a cultural transformation.

In 2019, a school district in Virginia implemented both an anti-racism policy and equity statement originally developed by students (Knott, 2018). The students wanted to alter the school's dress code policy. Their advocacy along with the creation of an ad hoc committee of concerned citizens birthed the creation of the anti-racism policy. The board's multifaceted policy denounced racism in school because it was antithetical to the district's mission, values, and goals. The robust policy included main principles and objectives along with a clear definition of the different types of racism. The assistant superintendent, Bernard Hairston, was quoted in the *Daily Progress* as saying, "By using the anti-racism policy to increase the racial consciousness of our staff, and to get them to understand the total impact of race, and at the same time we're applying our culture responsive teaching model, I think we're going to see some tremendous shifts in the next three to five years in our achievement gap data" (Knott, 2020). The policy was considered a tool to overall improve student outcomes.

The policy also addressed curriculum and instruction, training for staff, ways in which the policy would be enforced, and it required quarterly updates. As part of the policy implementation and communication, each campus was encouraged to post a public statement against racism. The statements were displayed in areas like the school's main office so it was visible to students, staff, and visitors (Albemarle County School District, 2019). It also added the policy language to the student handbook and was available in multiple languages. The policy also allowed for campuses to engage high school students in the efforts by serving on a diversity and equity committee. Specific charges were laid out for school administrators. They were charged with first modeling the behavior the school sought to achieve through the policy. Most notably, the board was responsible for implementing alternative discipline practices. Through the discipline reform, administrators were required to track and report all discipline data. When punitive action was taken against a student, there needed to be a written explanation of the behavior as well as details on the corrective action. Capturing this data helped further determine appropriate equitable interventions.

After a year of implementation, the policy underwent evaluation to assess its effectiveness. The Anti-Racism Policy Evaluation Report provided a snapshot on the progress of the issues outlined in the anti-racism policy in the short, intermediate, and long terms (2020). In the introduction of the report, the superintendent, Dr. Matthew S. Haas, wrote, "I used to believe that public schools—by virtue of their mere existence and without intention—would accomplish their charge to level the playing field for all children to reach their full potential. In reality, many of the structures we have in place in our schools—intentionally or unintentionally—perpetuate and enhance racial disparities against the mission we have to expand equity and inclusion." He also acknowledged that reducing racism is an ongoing process that will take some time before it is resolved. Still, this district was making strides in a new direction.

Within the first year of execution, the policy did make progress in many of the twenty-seven identified areas like reforming school discipline and creating subgroups to tackle the work collectively. However, other components required further cultivation like the hiring of more teachers of color to be more reflective of the student population. The goal was to hire twenty-five teachers of color annually. However, the district had only employed twenty teachers of color out of the 124 new hires (Knott, 2020). In an effort to develop more attractive recruitment strategies for teachers of color, the

Human Resources Department and the Office of Community Engagement began to work more collaboratively to figure out a solution (Policy Evaluation Report, 2020).

In closing, the Anti-Racism Policy Evaluation Report distinguished key lessons learned that can be useful for other districts interested in minimizing racism. Initially, everyone did not have the same level of understanding around anti-racism (2020). For many, it was also a difficult conversation to have. To decrease knowledge gaps on the topic, the district intentionally provided resources that included a district-wide book study on *Courageous Conversations About Race* accompanied by training tools on the subject. The district focused on capacity building by expanding its membership on several diversity and equity committees. This allowed for more diversity in ideas and creative ways to address issues. Lastly, high school students were key players in the work. All these components support systems change and can serve as a conduit for equity in education.

CHAPTER 5

THE PIONEERS OF SCHOOL POLICE IN TEXAS

——

When I began this writing journey, two facts were glaring, the first being that Black males were overly disciplined for their behaviors. Countless reports underscored that point. The second fact was that racial identity stood at the core of malpractice in school discipline across the nation. Moreover, according to the National Center for Education Statistics, about 65 percent of public schools, including charters, reported having the presence of a school resource officer on campus at least once a week (Dilliberti, et al., 2018). School-based police were one of the fastest-growing law enforcement segments according to the National Association of School Resource Officers (About NASRO, 2021). This organization develops training resources for thousands of law enforcement officers placed in schools. Data shows that students of color were frequently targeted in schools.

The aforementioned report from the National Center for Education Statistics took a look at crime and violence in schools. In the 2017–2018 school year, 51 percent of schools provided mental health assessments. Of those schools that provide assessments, only 38 percent offered treatment for the disorders. The disparity was startling to me because a vast number of students relied on schools as their primary access to mental health support. Similarly, the American School Counselor Association recommended a student-to-counselor ratio of 250 to one, but the national average was 424 to one. Not many school districts met the benchmark, and worse, some schools did not have a counselor at all. Still, budgets for police departments and law enforcement contracts remained healthy with 79 percent of schools having a sworn police officer on campus that carried a firearm (Dilliberti, et al., 2018).

Research has indicated school police officers were cogs in the school-to-prison pipeline, and data seemed to support that. The data was pointing to one narrative, but I was curious about how officers envisioned their roles in school. With that, I requested an interview with school assistant police chief, Marlon Runnels. Runnels immediately responded to my invitation, and he asked his superior officer, police chief David Kimberly, to join us. The district where the two officers served was the first school police department to be recognized by the state of Texas in 1982 (History). The interview was planned with one caveat. It would need to be scheduled three weeks out because Runnels coached his son's T-ball league. Honestly, this alleviated some of my personal apprehension about interacting with the police. At that moment I realized Runnels was also the parent of a Black son. It was possible that even as a member of law enforcement, he experienced some of the same fears for his child as I did for my son.

SCHOOL-BASED LAW ENFORCEMENT

I asked Runnels to describe himself and what had encouraged him to pursue a career in law enforcement. He shared that tragedy struck his family when he was nine years old. His father was senselessly murdered after winning a basketball game by one of the players on the opposite team. The police officer who delivered the devastating news emanated a compassionate demeanor to Runnels' family. This interaction inspired Runnels to become a police officer himself. He wanted to serve in a similar manner and play a protective yet empathetic role in the lives of others. With that in mind, he has had a career in law enforcement for fifteen years. He shared that during his time as a cadet in the police academy, the training did not particularly focus on school-based law enforcement, so when he first graduated he became a patrolman. For the past twelve years his law enforcement career has been in a school setting. When I asked what prompted the shift to work in schools, he simply replied he wanted a change of scenery.

Leaning in with empathy and reflecting on his experience as a young boy, he revealed, "One of the things I often share with my officers and my peers is every day we have the opportunity to change the narrative. A stigma is associated with law enforcement, within their subcategories. You have municipal agencies, you have county agencies, and then you have school-based policing. The perception is that school-based policing is a lower trained, or less attractive or less notable segment of policing. The reality is our officers particularly train, probably more than the average patrolmen you will see coming to your house—just because we are dealing with adolescence and everything that comes with that. We have a lot more state-mandated requirements."

Kimberly elaborated on the training requirements of the department he spearheads at the school district. Throughout the conversation, he rattled off numbers and statutory codes. He talked about training from the National Association of School Resource Officers, Texas Association of School Resources Officers, and the Texas Commission on Law Enforcement. What I found to be most interesting was an "Expectation Contract" he required police officers to sign. By doing so, the officer agreed to uphold the standards of the department. From what I was hearing, the department seemed exceptional in that they often developed their own curriculum to make sure officers could perform their jobs well. This was not always the case; the department has evolved over its thirty-nine years of existence.

Prior to 2015, Texas police officers located in school districts were not required to have youth-focused training. Legislation was passed for police officers located in schools with more than thirty-thousand students. To obtain licensure, police officers needed at least sixteen out of their forty training hours to have a focus on youth development. Smaller school districts that served under thirty thousand and had police on campus were exempt. Under the new policy officers had flexibility to decide between curriculum topics such as evidence-based conflict resolution training, child and adolescent psychology de-escalation techniques, and/or training on how to approach students with disabilities that have unique mental and behavioral needs (Texas State Legislature, 2015). The policy was poignant, but it would have been stronger if these foundational courses were requirements in addition to the forty hours. However, it was a step in the right direction considering police have been in schools for decades.

I wanted a better understanding of the distinction between school resource officers and school-based law enforcement. The terms were often used interchangeably but can differ significantly in many aspects. According to Kimberly, school resource officers can include sworn peace officers and those who have not taken any oaths. Yet the most noticeable difference is who each entity reports to. Police that contract with a school district report to the chief or sheriff of the local law enforcement agency. Police located within a school district, report to the superintendent similar to other campus leaders like principals do. He insinuated strong relationships were not built between officers and students when schools contracted with police. On the other hand, he felt school district police were seen as counselors, teachers, and/or mentors. He also perceived knowledge gaps and a lack of programs for adolescents as another variance between school districts that contracted with local law enforcement.

ELEMENTS FOR EQUITY

I scrutinized their school district's code of conduct to understand at what point police were brought into situations. In taking a closer look, the code of conduct handbook stated, "Disciplinary action will draw on the professional judgment of teachers and administrators and a range of disciplinary techniques" (Student Code of Conduct: 2020–2021). I found this statement to be problematic if educators were not trained in areas that enhanced competence in handling discipline or taught to examine cultural bias around race and other identities. I was curious if there was a clear distinction in which party handled school discipline—administrators or police. This curiosity was sparked by a report from Texas Appleseed that suggested school discipline was more often dispensed in a criminal format by police officers than in a restorative way by administrators. The report suggested this occurred when administrators were overwhelmed or not properly informed about how to resolve the student misconduct.

Another statement in the school code of conduct added that disciplinary action was also contingent upon "the seriousness of the offense, the student's age and grade level, the frequency, the student's attitude, the effect the misconduct had on the school environment and statutory requirements" (Student Code of Conduct: 2020–2021). This language appeared vague and open to discretion. It was also potentially problematic because research pointed out that Black students were more likely to be disciplined although Black students were not more likely to misbehave than their counterparts (Rudd, 2012). Black students were highly disciplined for subjected actions deemed deviant like "disrespecting" a teacher or "talking back." Factors like "the student's attitude" seemed impossible to fairly assess. Furthermore, Rudd's research supported that when given the opportunity to select severe disciplinary consequences for small incidents, teachers and administrators often choose the most extreme punishment for Black students.

The code of conduct outlined examples of four levels of offenses. The lowest level included behavior such as being tardy, not following classroom rules set by the teacher, misusing food in the cafeteria, or using a cell phone in class. The offenses included issues like chewing gum, violating the dress code, disrupting class, or participating in a sit-in or boycott. This violation stood out to me given that many relationships between law enforcement and schools began because of protests and boycotts about unfair treatment of students of color during the Civil Rights Era. The highest level of infractions were egregious activities that were illegal by nature. This encompassed carrying a weapon, murder, robbery, or selling or possessing drugs and controlled substances. All the aforementioned violations could result in a myriad of disciplinary measures, from school detention to arrests, even for nonviolent offenses.

I asked Kimberly at what point police were brought into school code of conduct violations. A common misconception is that police are often brought into situations as a very last resort. Another is that police are brought in when there is imminent danger that threatens safety. Kimberly's response was, "That varies. It can be never or at the very beginning." He was adamant that police should not be part of school discipline and that policies and statutory codes explicitly forbade it. In my research I saw countless examples of police utilized as an integral part of school discipline. Runnels clarified, "We try to discern the difference between formal and informal interactions with our students for our officers. When they're wearing their formal hat, that means a criminal offense has occurred and we're coming in a law enforcement role to investigate and deal with the situation from that lens." He also shared there are informal interactions where they can positively engage students because of the relationships they build.

My final question to the two officers was about the recommendation to end the relationship with school law enforcement by the American Federation of Teachers. Runnels was the only one who offered his opinion. "Personally, I think it is a short-sighted knee-jerk type of response to the situations that have been occurring. Especially when all it really takes is a kind of conversation with those agencies, if you are contracting with them, on what you want to see or what policing should look like in your school. There are good models, and I can pat ourselves on the back and say that we're probably one of the good models. So, if you truly value school safety and you truly value those relationships, just have a conversation to change what that looks like so it fits your needs and expectations." When I had more time to reflect on his answer and this emphasis on relationships, it reminded me of the idea of restorative justice.

As it stands, many school police officers play a pivotal role in the school-to-prison-pipeline because law enforcement is a component of a deeply rooted system that manufactured inequity since way before the Civil Rights Era. School police often act in response to situations that first involve a school district staff person, like a teacher or assistant principal. It's a flawed system that needs to be innovated. Kimberly admitted research-driven reports had highlighted his school district's dreadful discipline policies in the past. He understood the impact his department had on students and made the decision to take action. "I think campus administration over utilized us for things so that pendulum swung way out there somewhere around 2003 to 2004. I saw it. I was working with Appleseed and some of the groups. I saw what was going on, and that's why these curriculum and innovations have become so important. Let's remake or re-envision what a campus officer looks like."

A SINGLE BULLET

Two weeks after the interview with Kimberly and Runnels, a seventeen-year-old Black student, Anthony J. Thompson, Jr., was reported as being killed by police at his high school in Knoxville, Tennessee. The student had brought a gun to school and local law enforcement was called to the campus. During the situation, officers had ordered the student to exit the restroom stall where he had locked himself in (Rojas, 2021). When I think of my experience as a seventeen-year-old, I imagine the student was probably afraid. He probably had not fully comprehended the gravity of his situation. He had a lapse in judgement that ended in deadly ramifications.

On the body-camera footage of an officer, Thompson can be seen trying to possibly break free from the police while being apprehended (Brown, 2021). Police reacted to the struggle, and within seconds Thompson was killed by a single bullet. An officer was also wounded by gunshot, but it was later reported that his injury was the result of a fellow officer. The bullet was not from Thompson's gun. In the video, another student can be seen in the restroom. One officer drew his gun and pointed it directly at this student while ordering him to get to the ground. The student was then handcuffed but can be heard pleading with the officers to help Thompson who was lifelessly handcuffed as he bled to death.

On that day, another Black life was lost at the hands of police. A bad decision had turned into a tragic day of mourning. I'm not privy to any additional background information about Anthony J. Thompson. I also do not condone bringing a gun into a school building. Reflecting on my conversation with Runnels, a man who had lost his own father to gun violence,

I wondered how his skills as a trained negotiator would have helped him handle the Thompson situation. Being a Black man, in a situation involving a Black student, I honestly believe he would have had empathy. Even given only a split second to make a decision, I think he would have figured out a way to handle it so Thompson remained alive.

Throughout our interview Kimberly framed many of his responses by asking the question, "If that were your kid, what would you want to see happen?" My answer was invariably that I would want my Black son to be extended the same grace as his White peers. The same grace given to a White supremacist that murdered people worshipping at a church in Charleston, South Carolina. The same due process offered a White male after he made the decision to kill protestors who denounced police brutality in Kenosha, Wisconsin. I would want my son to be accountable for any wrongdoings but most importantly, I would want my son to be alive.

CHAPTER 6

EVERYTHING CHANGED IN EIGHT MINUTES AND FORTY-SIX SECONDS

————

On May 25, 2020, Houston Independent School District alumnus George Floyd was heinously murdered by the Minneapolis Police Department. For eight minutes and forty-six seconds, an officer of the law obstructed Floyd's breathing. In between gasps for air, he pleaded for his life. He eventually died less than nine minutes later. Floyd left behind his young daughter and other family and friends who loved and cherished him.

His death was not the first murder at the hands of the police. However, it impacted me more personally because a close friend of mine had attended high school with him in Houston. I grieved his unnecessary loss with my friend, sharing in her pain. Images and videos of his death flooded my social media timelines, the twenty-four-hour news cycle, and even my text messages. I remember reading a statement from the Houston Independent School District Interim Superintendent referring to his death as an "unconscionable loss." The statement was short, but in the end, she expressed hope for meaningful change (Lathan, 2020).

This event compounded the high anxiety I was already experiencing from the COVID-19 pandemic. Floyd's untimely death sparked a new surge of urgency for equitable treatment of all Americans. It drew much-needed attention to the long-standing perils of police brutality and lethality in Black communities. Protesters across the nation occupied many public spaces calling for systemic reforms around racism and anti-Blackness. Crucial conversations about race, equity, and oppression were had across all sectors like corporate board rooms, nonprofit organizations, and other institutions. On my end, I facilitated conversations with community organizers and coalition partners with the goal to reform the Houston Independent School District Police Department. The work was personal to me because it would be the school district my son attended.

In many education spaces, there was new curiosity about the presence of police officers in schools as it related to school discipline. According to a report titled, "Bullies in Blue: The Origins and Consequences of School Policing," the presence of police on campuses typically commanded authority because they have the power to arrest. The report also suggested the presence of police often escalated disciplinary situations that would otherwise be considered minute, like talking back to an officer or walking away. In many cases where school police were brought into disciplinary circumstances, it led to students being criminalized for adolescent behaviors that irritate or antagonize adults. As turbulent as that behavior may be, it was not illegal. On top of that, schools with a majority Black and Hispanic population not only were more likely to have police on campus, but Black students were also twice as likely to get arrested than their White counterparts (King and Lhamon, 2015).

REIMAGINING POLICE-FREE SCHOOLS ACROSS THE NATION

I found the energy that bubbled in America around the role of police a much-needed conversation starter. It made me realize police who had beats in local neighborhoods could also be the very same officers who patrol schools. Prior to the multiple protests, I found it slightly difficult to imagine school halls that lacked the presence of police officers. The relationship between law enforcement and schools had spanned over decades. Police were a fixture in many schools especially in urban communities. But times were changing!

After the death of George Floyd, by June 2, the *Star Tribune* had reported that the Minneapolis School Board unanimously voted to end its $1.1 million contract for services with the Minneapolis Police Department. This entity had practically served as school resources officers in their middle and high school buildings for eons. The superintendent charged the board with coming up with a new plan for safety for the next school year (Faircloth, 2020). The resolution had unwavering support from its trustees, but there were mixed feelings from stakeholders about the new direction of Minneapolis schools. People wondered about safety despite the lack of research supporting the idea that police made schools safer.

Within that same week, Mayor of Portland Ted Wheeler announced that police would be removed from Portland Public Schools. In a press conference, the mayor ordered the immediate removal of police and reallocated funds to "disrupt the patterns of racism and injustice" (Riski, 2020). Neighboring school districts, David Douglas and Parkrose School Districts followed suit and removed police from patrolling their high schools as well. This was not the first attempt at removing police from schools. In the past, the issue did not garner enough support for school board trustees to vote in favor of the change. With the new measure in place, the superintendent of Portland Public Schools wanted to invest more in student supports like counselors and social workers.

Conversations about police-free schools were happening at large urban school districts like the Los Angeles Unified School District. For years, advocacy groups throughout Los Angeles campaigned for police reforms and/or police-free schools. The Los Angeles School Police Department held the title of the largest independent police district. It ranked eighth largest in Los Angeles County and the fourteenth largest police department in California (LA School Police / Los Angeles School Police Department, 2019). In 2019, the department employed 211 sworn police officers, twenty-five non-sworn officers who served as school resource officers, and thirty-two civilian support staff. In an analysis of the department between 2014 and 2017, police arrested 3,389 students, issued 2,724 ticket citations, and referred 1,282 students to diversion programs (Allen et, al., 2017). The vast majority of these students were students of color. This is likely the reason so many students were against having police in their schools for years (Kohl, 2020).

Of the aforementioned infractions, Black youth comprised a whopping 25 percent of those incidents but only represented a mere 9 percent of the student population (Allen et al., 2017). I could only imagine the surmounting challenges Black students must have faced trying to get an education. The school police were also heavily armed. During that same three-year period, the *Los Angeles Times* reported the school police department received federal grants to purchase military-grade weapons. Those weapons included armored vehicles, rifles, and grenade launchers (Ceasar, 2020). Oddly enough, none of these items belonged in schools and the department eventually returned the grenade launchers. It's no wonder that in 2020, United Teachers Los Angeles, with a membership of over thirty-thousand, voted in support of eliminating the Los Angeles School Police Department's seventy-million-dollar budget (Kohli, 2020).

According to a *Los Angeles Times* article, the United Teachers Los Angeles president believed that the seventy million dollars of the police's budget could be used to hire eight hundred mental health employees (Kholi and Blume, 2020). In place of the police, the teachers union recommended more counselors and restorative justice programs. After seven months of research and deliberation, the Los Angeles Unified School District voted to replace officers with staff who were trained in conflict resolution and knew how to de-escalate situations with students.

The board's new policy eliminated 133 police positions and reduced the police department budget by twenty-five million dollars. New staff under the title of School Climate Coach were trained on topics like understanding implicit bias and how to strengthen student engagement through social-emotional learning (Shuttleworth, 2021). Other policy changes included banning the use of pepper spray on students by police officers. The change also required oversight and accountability in how the police department operated. Schools were also given an assessment tool to use when requesting a police presence on campus (Board of Education of the City of Los Angeles, 2020). This new tool was a game-changer for school staff because it helped determine the difference between discipline issues and criminal matters.

The board also approved thirty-six million dollars dedicated to the Black Student Achievement Plan (Shuttleworth, 2021). This initiative provided additional support to fifty-three campuses with higher enrollments of Black students (Board of Education of the City of Los Angeles, 2020). It also looked at other campus indicators like high discipline referral rates and suspension rates. As a parent, I felt this priority was especially important because the Department of Education Office of Civil Rights surveyed all public schools during the 2013–2014 school year (King and Lhamon, 2015). The data found that racial disparities in suspensions were apparent and that Black boys were nearly four times more likely to receive a suspension compared to White students. Also, Black boys were nearly two times more likely to be expelled and referred to law enforcement.

The goal of the Black Student Achievement Plan addressed three facets that support more equitable education for Black students. The first ensured the curriculum was culturally responsive and provided interventions to address gaps in literacy and math. The second was to partner with community groups that have built relationships with Black students and families. Lastly, it aimed to reduce the over-identification of Black students being disciplined through interventions and social-emotional learning. It was a great stride toward educational equity.

After having a presence of police on campus for nearly forty years, the Los Angeles Unified School District disrupted an oppressive system by eliminating their police department. Bold leaders at the Los Angeles Unified School District were able to imagine an education system that worked for all students. This seismic shift in policy toward equity could potentially alter academic outcomes and narrow achievement gaps for many students. More importantly, the new changes simply treated students like humans and not hardened criminals.

"ONCE WE HAVE SYSTEMS IN PLACE, WE GET USED TO THEM."

In Colorado, the Denver Education Board followed similar action as other school districts in response to the murder of George Floyd. On June 12, their board voted to reduce its police force by 25 percent and fully sever its relationship with law enforcement the following school year (Quinton, 2020). For years, civil rights advocates, along with some parents and various students, called for change. The civil unrest around police brutality in the nation was the motivation for transformation. The Denver Education Board advocated to reallocate funds toward student resources. The district wanted to hire social workers, psychologists, and behavior specialists. Another component of the policy change was a proposal to create a monthly school discipline report.

While the public called for expeditious change, school leaders like principals and deans championed a slower phase-out of school police in Denver. The Denver Police Department was on contract with the school district and the resolution did not impact public safety officers who were considered school employees (Quinton, 2020). However, school safety was still an important issue, and the resolution created a partnership to help formulate a plan to address student security. The plan required figuring out how to utilize police as a very last resort.

With Denver Public Schools as early adopters of police-free campuses, I reached out to Angela Cobian, treasurer of the Denver Board of Education, to learn more about this seemingly impossible movement. Before we got into our conversation, I wanted to know what motivated her to serve on the school board. She told me a story about her life as a young student where she and two of her friends were confronted by White students who belonged to a Confederate flag-toting, White supremacy group in school. I know how difficult this must have been to have to deal with overt racism in school.

Being of Mexican heritage, Cobian recalled the White students had yelled racial slurs at her and her friends. She had responded with the same forceful language. Amid the hurling of objectionable epithets, the student had demanded they fight at the end of the school week. She admitted to being terrified because she had never had a physical altercation before. At the time of the incident, she was also the secretary of the Student Government Association and did not want to put her academic career in jeopardy.

She confided with the SGA's group advisor about the looming fight because she was a trusted adult. They had built a relationship through the program. When Cobian provided details about the situation, the advisor knew exactly who the antagonizing student was. This was the student's third altercation using racially offensive language toward students of color. The student was expelled from school, and the fight never happened. Cobian felt she escaped a dreadful situation.

"A presence that made me feel unsafe and unwelcome at school was removed which in hindsight is also crazy because as someone who believes in restorative justice—I'm not sure if three strikes you're out of school is the way to go. But in that moment, it did so much for me. I still ended up staying in school. I stayed in student government. I joined the debate team. I did all these really healthy activities that kept me wanting to stay in school. That helped me explore and find my passion and develop myself. But in one moment, if I would not have asked for help, if I would have gotten into that fight, I just don't know where I would be right now." In that heartfelt story, she had also mentioned that by age fourteen, many of her friends from middle school had already dropped out of school.

We shifted the conversation to modern times because I wanted to know if the murder of George Floyd was the reason the Denver Board of Education made the rather quick decision to remove police from schools. It certainly appeared that way from my perspective based on the timeline of events. However, according to her, a community organizing group called Padres & Jovenes Unidos, (translated in English to mean "Parents and Students United") had been advocating for this policy change for a decade. This organization worked toward a myriad of issues such as racial justice, equity in education, and immigration issues (Home, 2020). Police reform had only been one of their larger undertakings.

Cobian lamented, "His very public murder, I would say, created the momentum to do it once and for all. I have a lot of feelings about that in hindsight because, you know, on the one hand, it's like I said, people have been organizing for this for years. Why did it take the public execution of a man for us to do this? But on the other hand, it's like why don't we listen to organizing groups more regularly. And why does it take something so awful for us to move quickly?"

In the past, organizing groups had presented the idea of removing police from schools at many board meetings but the effort did not have enough support. This has been the case in Los Angeles, Minneapolis, Oakland, and many other places. Yet since the murder of George Floyd, several school districts have ended their relationships with law enforcement. In doing so, districts freed up millions of dollars in their budgets, according to the Justice Policy Institute (Harris, 2020).

At the time of our interview, the Denver Public School district was without police in schools for a year. I wanted to know if the removal of police had an impact on students. I surmised students probably felt safer in the hallways and that arrests were down. Cobian shared, "Ending our contract with the police department, as quickly as we did, had had a lot of consequences that I don't think we foresaw because we believed so much in what we were doing at the time. I think we were like, 'We'll deal with the consequences as they come.'"

With any drastic change, unforeseen circumstances were common. She went on to say, "For example, this program that we had with the police department, it was to have school resource officers in eighteen of our high schools. Meanwhile, there are 225 schools in DPS. It was a really small program to begin with, and all but one [of the police officers] were officers of color from the communities they were serving." By removing police from schools, the district had unintentionally eliminated the jobs of people of color. That was important considering the COVID-19 pandemic had caused a surge in unemployment rates (Data Tables, 2021).

Another subsequent challenge Cobian outlined was that many communities in Denver were plagued by gun violence and relied on police to keep communities safe. Over the years, gun violence in Colorado had become so extreme that elected officials introduced legislation to establish an Office of Gun Violence Prevention (Office of Gun Violence Prevention, 2021). She expressed some of the concern from citizens: "So another thing that we heard was there's so much gun violence in the neighborhood and now you're moving police from schools. You're not going to keep our kids safe." I understood both sides of this issue. When I attended school, crime was a serious problem in many Chicago neighborhoods. However, the solution to that problem in the 1990s was more police in schools and metal detectors, which proved ineffective (Kunichoff, 2017).

I hoped Denver Public Schools would not adopt a similar framework to curtail community violence after working so diligently toward progress. Instead, the district leaned into its obstacles and sought out other ways to address safety concerns. Cobian indicated, "It's an opportunity for us to radically change the way we think of safety. Because we rely on the police after a crime has already happened, like a shooting. Or at a school, we rely on police after an incident at a grave level happens. But that means we're only ever responding. We're not preventing anything. We are constantly treating the symptoms and not the problem."

In the Denver Public Schools resolution to remove police from schools, another component aimed to reallocate $721,000 of the police budget toward support for students (Quinton, 2020). Cobian declared, "It's going to take way more than $700,000 to reimagine safety." She then mentioned a program a student group wanted to pilot that cost three million dollars. The pilot would have a centralized team of mental health counselors. Their sole focus would be mental health and therapy for students. "When we think about what it's going to take to rethink safety in schools. It's going to require a long-term, sustained investment of resources."

Cobian also brought up why it's important to have diverse mental health workers. She believed they should be reflective of the school demographics and include people of color and Spanish speakers. She suggested counselors should also be trained in culturally responsive pedagogy. Cobian emphasized that achieving diversity required building a pipeline of qualified mental health workers through partnerships with universities. This seemed like a simple way to recruit the right people for the roles.

In our conversation I recognized that only a limited number of school districts have removed the presence of police from campuses. I believe that number will continue to increase as more groups organize around this matter. I felt it necessary to hear her thoughts on why so few schools had made the shift. I shared with her a bit of my disappointment about the Houston Independent School District not making police reforms. Their police were allowed to pepper spray students and my son was going to attend kindergarten in that school district. The thought of that honestly scared me.

"The reality is that once we have systems in place, we become used to them. And we think that's all that can exist. It's actually really hard for people to reimagine and rethink systems after they have gotten used to them. I would push school board members to leverage their power position, to be the ones to push for that reimagining because our schools need all of those preventative investments in their mental and physical safety that are going to enable them to be successful." We both believed students deserve and need those resources. Moreover, students are impacted by these school policies, and their voices should be centered in discussions around these issues.

MENTAL HEALTH RESOURCES IN SCHOOLS
Students spend the bulk of their day in school buildings. During that time, multiple things happen at once. Students engage in a new curriculum while simultaneously retaining information from other subjects. Students may interact with other youth and adults from different backgrounds in class or via extracurricular activities. Students may think about what's happening in the moment as well as their future endeavors. Some may be processing trauma they experienced

at home. Others may be a split second away from making a life-changing decision. For those reasons, educational institutions should more aggressively provide mental health resources in schools to support the positive development of young people.

Furthermore, there is a growing reliance on schools to support students beyond academics because mental health disorders have increased over time. It is estimated by the National Survey of Children's Health that one in six youth meet the criteria for a diagnosable mental health disorder (Whitney and Peterson, 2019). This data was determined from the analysis of over forty-six million students across the nation. Unfortunately, on a national scale, only about half received the care they needed. Over time, mental health problems become exacerbated. This impacts students' grades, as well as how they behave in schools.

Often, these diagnoses come from school-based mental health workers such as counselors or school psychologists. Lower income students have greater barriers of connection to these resources outside of school for multiple reasons such as a lack of health insurance. Schools have a unique opportunity to shift how students experience mental health or illness by providing the services on campus. Some families may also feel more comfortable accessing these supports in a setting they are familiar with (School-Based Mental Health, 2021). It's also an opportunity to build trust and buy-in from parents and caregivers.

In 2021, the American Academy of Pediatrics examined seven highly functioning school districts that implemented a school-based mental health program. The comprehensive model included seven features: "well-trained educators and specialized instructional support, family-school-community collaboration and teaming, multi-tiered system support, mental health screening, evidence-based and emerging practices, data and funding" (Supporting Mental Health in Schools, 2021). By implementing all seven features, the program was wildly successful. For starters, principles of equity were a critical component of the program and fostered conversations about anti-racism in mental health services. Equity teams and diversity councils were formed, and leaders were mindful in selecting the right staff to help develop the program. Those staff were dedicated to achieving equity for all students.

The implementation was nuanced among districts because they vastly varied in size, location, and student population. However, common points of progress among the seven districts included starting small and scaling up after making improvements throughout the program. Schools typically had a district-level administrator champion the program that trickled down to individual campuses. Relationships and partnerships were built outside of the school building to provide the mental health services students needed (Supporting Mental Health in Schools, 2021). Engaging different stakeholders with unique perspectives provided a solid foundation for the school districts to implement the program. Over time, the initiative was no longer seen as a program, but as a fiber of the school's culture.

Above all, schools should invest in mental health resources so students have a positive experience on campus. It is a way schools can address racial inequities in mental health access and school discipline referrals. Comprehensive mental health programs in schools help students academically as well as support development in building social skills and caring connections to adults (School-Based Mental Health, 2021). It does take time and resources to develop the new infrastructure, but it is worth it for the students and the students deserve it.

CHAPTER 7

WHAT EXACTLY IS RESTORATIVE JUSTICE?

During the COVID-19 pandemic, my place of work went completely remote, and I began working from home. There was so much uncertainty about the virus that I decided to remove my son from preschool as a precaution. Local school districts had also closed their doors and begun implementing virtual learning. The following fall, some school districts had reopened their buildings for teachers but not yet for students. Educational institutions were forced to rapidly change to adapt to the shifting needs of the community.

My sister-in-law taught kindergarten and was required to deliver her remote instruction for her students from the actual classroom. However, her daughter, who attended the same school as a first grader, was not allowed to enter the school building because of liability reasons. When I could, I would babysit my niece while her parents worked. It was nice because my son needed a playmate from time to time.

In between Zoom calls, I would hear the two of them bickering, a precursor that soon escalated to screaming and then someone crying. On one day in particular there was an argument over a Spider-Man toy. Even though my son had hundreds of Spider-Men and other toys my niece wanted to play with that particular toy at that moment. According to my son, he had the toy first and decided to pry the toy from my niece's hand. She pushed him; he fell and started to cry.

Because I only had five minutes before my next obligation, I was prepared to put them both in time out as a quick solution. But as the two retold their story through tears I felt compelled to listen to understand. I asked how each person felt about what had happened and how we could fix it so we all could have fun. I watched as a four- and six-year-old expressed accountability, remorse, and a promise to play together nicely moving forward. After our conversation ended the two went into the room to play again. I could overhear laughter, joyful banter, and my son offering to allow his cousin to play with his toys first. Unknowingly, I had facilitated the practice of restorative justice before my next Zoom meeting.

The Zehr Institute for Restorative Justice believes that while the philosophies of restorative justice began eons ago, it was introduced to the western world in the 1970s to address weaknesses in the punitive legal system. "Recognizing that punishment is often ineffective, restorative justice aims at helping offenders to recognize the harm they have caused and encouraging them to repair the harm, to the extent it is possible. Rather than obsessing about whether offenders get what they deserve, restorative justice focuses on repairing the harm of crime and engaging individuals and community members in the process" (Zehr Institute, 2021). In the case of restorative justice in schools, it enlists students to be part of the process of restoration. Students utilize this technique to solve problems that traditionally trigger a punitive response from school administrators.

A 2019 report by WestEd Justice and Prevention Research Center postulated that restorative justice programs became popular in American schools to address the negative impact that exclusionary discipline had on students. The report cited this was due to zero-tolerance discipline policies that took root in the 1990s (Fronius et al., 2019). Those policies often increased the usage of exclusionary discipline and suspensions. To counter that practice, restorative justice programs were utilized as a solution to address exclusionary discipline. It aimed to handle the misbehavior in a manner that did not remove students from their school setting. This was important because the report examined data from studies on school discipline that noted that Black students were 26 percent more likely to receive a suspension than their White counterparts (Fronius et al., 2019).

RESTORATIVE JUSTICE IN URBAN SCHOOLS

In Walter H. Dyett High School, a Chicago Public School located on the Chicago Southside, implemented a successful youth-led restorative justice program. According to research from the Collaborative for Equity and Justice in Education, between 1999 and 2012, Dyett High School experienced numerous challenges. When the school converted from a middle school to a high school it offered no Advanced Placement or Honors courses for students. The school also did not have adequate resources to support its special education students which comprised over 25 percent of the student body (Gutierrez et, al., 2012).

There was not a shortage of challenges plaguing this community. The report portrayed a dismal environment for students, stating that the building facilities were deteriorating and had issues with heating, air conditioning, and plumbing. The school also experienced extreme turnover in school leadership, only being able to maintain a principal for a short while. Enrichment programs were constantly cut due to budget constraints, including their restorative justice program (Gutierrez et, al., 2012). Concurrently, violence in the school and community soared. The report suggested this was due to the removal of public housing and neighborhood re-gentrification.

Still, people organized and advocated for change. With the school on the brink of closing, Dyett's Local School Council developed a new restorative justice program. This replaced the one that was initially defunded as the school's resources diminished (Gutierrez et al., 2012). After the turnaround, a group called the Safe and Supportive Consortium developed a training manual to help educators implement restorative justice programs in their classrooms. The shift was effective in many ways and contributed to a districtwide change in suspensions. In the 2013–2014 school year, The University of Chicago conducted a study that showed suspensions decreased to 16 percent mainly because of shifts in discipline options (Allensworth et al., 2015).

By 2015, the Chicago school district had rewritten the school code of conduct and implemented restorative justice programs at more campuses. In a *Chicago Tribune* article the recording secretary of the Chicago Teachers Union, Michael Brunson, shared, "It's difficult to go from a zero-tolerance mentality to a restorative justice mentality because it's a whole different way of looking at things. To really do restorative justice, there have to be certain things in place" (Perez, 2019). In the same article, some teachers from various campuses voiced their complaints about feeling ill-equipped to deal with disruptive students. Their gripes were justifiable because restorative justice required a commitment to the process as well as an allocation of time and money. A restorative justice culture does not happen overnight.

Still, some schools across the nation have adopted the practice of restorative justice to mitigate punitive discipline practices. Oakland Unified School Districts was one of the first in the nation to implement the program in schools. In 2007, Restorative Justice for Oakland Youth wanted to "engage families, communities, and systems to repair harm and prevent re-offending" (Restorative Justice for Oakland Youth, 2021). They pitched the program to Alameda County's Juvenile Court and other juvenile justice stakeholders. The presentation emphasized how restorative justice could reduce racial disparities in discipline. This was a compounding issue in Oakland schools. But by implementing restorative justice programs, there could be diminished rates of incarceration, suspension, and expulsion according to Restorative Justice for Oakland Youth. The presiding juvenile court judge then convened a Restorative Justice Task Force, and the beginning of the program was born.

The purpose of the task force was to develop avenues to divert youth from the juvenile justice system altogether. It aimed to create community-based sentencing alternatives and circles of support for youth re-entering their schools and communities after incarceration. The vision of the task force was to create a "juvenile justice system that is improved by county-wide restorative practices which emphasizes repairing the harm caused by youthful wrongdoing while reducing the social and financial cost of our present system" (Alameda County Restorative Juvenile Justice Strategic Plan, 2012). Members of the task force created a three-year implementation plan that focused on capacity building, training, and pilot projects at specific schools. Cole Middle School in West Oakland was the restorative justice program school pioneer (Tepperman, 2013). Within one year, that campus reduced the school's suspension rates by an overwhelming 87 percent. The preliminary program was working!

Inspired in part by the dramatic reduction in suspensions, the Oakland Unified School District Board signed a resolution to implement a districtwide restorative justice framework (Resolution of the Board of Education Oakland Unified School District, 2009). Resources were allocated to promote equitable discipline policies that did not solely concentrate on punitive practices. Similar to the planning of the task force, the district created a three-year implementation plan that required training and professional development for school staff including its police department. Local campuses were also granted the flexibility to create their own policies as long as they did not conflict with the original tenets of restorative justice resolution.

These restorative changes were necessary. Before these shifts, the Oakland Unified School District data showed Black students were being disciplined at greater rates than their counterparts. This triggered an investigation by the United States Department of Education Office of Civil Rights on whether Black students were disciplined more frequently and harshly than White students. As a remedy, the school district entered a voluntary resolution settlement with the Department of Education. By doing so, the district agreed to utilize an alternative approach to discipline that did not include suspensions to address misbehavior. It opted to implement restorative justice programs.

Another agreement of the settlement included reviewing and revising codes of conduct and disciplinary policies. Students with behavior challenges were provided more resources to ensure they were still able to learn if removed from their classrooms for behavioral reasons. There was a concerted effort to communicate the changes to parents and other stakeholders. Their input was solicited via survey as well as other elements that collected school discipline data. The district then used survey responses to figure out what reforms were necessary to meet the unique and diverse needs of the community.

A lot of change was happening in California in relation to school discipline. In 2012, Governor Jerry Brown, signed into law Assembly Bill 1729, a piece of legislation that provided authorization of school leaders to use age-appropriate alternatives to suspensions or expulsions to correct misconduct. This effort relaxed outdated zero-tolerance discipline policies. Schools were encouraged to seek more flexible solutions like tiered interventions or participation in a restorative justice program. It required leaders to think of other options besides traditional suspension or expulsion that removed students from schools.

Community groups like the Black Organizing Project and the American Civil Liberties Union of Northern California championed the shift toward restorative justice (Frey, 2015). By 2015, Oakland Unified School District invested $2.3 million in restorative justice programming and removed "willful defiance" as a reason for suspending students. This was monumental because, in the 2013–2014 school year, Black students had accounted for over 50 percent of the suspensions for reasons of "disturbance or willful defiance." At the time Black students represented only 25 percent of the student population (Frey, 2015).

Over the span of a decade, the district had shifted its policies, systems, and environment. The Oakland Unified School District focused on a restorative way to address student behavior. Eventually, the district experienced reduced suspensions, expulsions, and decreased arrests for students. By 2020, the school board passed the George Floyd Resolution to Eliminate the Oakland Schools Police Department (Reilly, 2020). This transitioned law enforcement out of schools and allowed the district to hire more restorative justice practitioners.

RESTORATIVE JUSTICE IS LIKE THE HEART OF A CAMPUS

In early 2020, before the world shut down all normal activities due to the COVID-19 virus, I had the opportunity to conduct a site visit at a charter high school in Houston to see a restorative justice program in action. I was invited by Dr. Anita Wadhwa who served as the restorative justice coordinator. Her research-based strategies for schools to implement restorative justice programs resulted in higher academic achievement and better behavior from students.

She brought a wealth of expertise to the subject of restorative justice. As the author of *Restorative Justice in Urban Schools: Disrupting the School to Prison Pipeline*, she examined the historical context of the school-to-prison pipeline. She also founded a consulting agency that empowers youth with the support of adults to co-facilitate restorative justice training. I wanted to interview Dr. Wadhwa to determine why her high school campus had been so accomplished in their restorative justice programs, but neighboring school districts were stagnant and invested more resources in law enforcement than mental health resources.

When asked what brought her to the practice of restorative justice her response was based on emotional empathy. She reflected on her experience as a student when she felt marginalized in school while dealing with undiagnosed mental health issues. When she was younger her family moved from Houston to a predominantly White town in Ohio where she was one of three students of color in the entire school. She shared that feeling marginalized "deeply impacts your ability to love people, how you communicate, how you navigate the world, and how successful you can be." She further added that feeling marginalized in schools can have an even greater impact on students beyond the classroom.

We spoke about discipline and the negative connection associated with the word. Mental health resources appeared to be an afterthought as many schools across the nation simply lacked staff like counselors. This often led to punishment that was not restorative. "I don't think the word 'discipline' is bad. Obviously, we don't want to be punitive. I just want to emphasize when I talk about it because people think restorative justice is soft and cuddly. People listen and then people do whatever they want to do. No! Everyone has to feel respected so that when you walk away if there's harm, you have to walk away and see things change to actually feel like harm has been repaired." I was understanding restorative justice should be a component of discipline.

I let her words sink in and thought about how difficult it was for me to admit when I was harmed or when I may have harmed others in school. Pondering on her words took me back to high school when I was suspended for ten days. From that moment on I carried a pang of heavy guilt and shame about the entire situation. I had locked away a part of who I was, but in this conversation with Dr. Wadhwa, I felt free from the guilt and shame I carried with me since high school. In hindsight, the school should have provided different options to address the situation for all the students instead of simply suspending everyone.

A feeling of liberation surfaced when she shared how restorative justice can be central to the mental health and well-being of young learners. It gets to the root of what causes trauma or factors outside of the classroom that are a catalyst for misconduct. Many schools across the country were making adjustments in policies and programs, and this made me hopeful. Some schools were trying to understand why students misbehave instead of just punishing them.

I asked Dr. Wadhwa if she honestly believed all schools could implement restorative justice programs given the constraints of time and need for other resources. From my research, it had taken schools like Oakland Unified School

District well over ten years to reach a point of success. She answered in the affirmative and stated, "It should begin with adult leaders on campus like administrators and teachers. Adults would have to shift their mindsets to be more restorative and adopt a belief that being punitive is not the only way to discipline students. Then students should be brought into the process."

In terms of how long a school-wide shift to restorative justice should take, she mentioned, "If you're building up a new campus you can have a fully restorative school in a year. But if you're going into a traditional campus that's trying to make some changes, I think three to five years—knowing that it should be a lifelong move." A report from the WestEd Justice and Prevention Research Center, reinforced that timeframe, stating that successful implementation could take up to five years, but various factors are involved, like the size of the school. The program becomes more sustainable when integrated into school policy and procedures and not viewed as an alternative to discipline.

She admitted some schools would have to be innovative in funding the program. "It's more of a failure of creativity than a failure of budget or lack of time" she argued. An effective restorative justice program would require a coordinator to oversee the program and conduct training. However, Dr. Wadhwa did say that a school could start with a part-time position or a contract employee. She even suggested training the staff person who usually oversees the in-school suspension room. While I agreed this person was already on staff, I was not sure if he/she could easily adopt a new mindset of restorative justice.

On the whole, her ideas were very sound, and although I've never had the privilege of serving in a classroom, I found them to be reasonable. When our conversation ended, I felt empowered because I believed restorative justice was feasible if there is empathy for students. On the day when I felt triumphant in implementing restorative justice during my Zoom call, my success was attributed to the fact that I loved both my son and my niece. I wanted the outcome of the situation to equitably work out for both of them. Restorative justice can work in schools if we emanate love for all students.

CHAPTER 8

RACISM IS A PUBLIC HEALTH MATTER AND SO IS EXCLUSIONARY DISCIPLINE

———

Racism is defined as a "system consisting of structures, policies, practices, and norms—that assigns value and determines opportunity based on the way people look or the color of their skin" (Racism and Health, 2021). Because of that, many communities across the nation have recognized racism as a public health matter. It may seem odd to think of racism as a health issue, but racism has had a negatively profound impact on people of color, which has also included adverse experiences in schools. Striving for equity would create prosperity for everyone instead of unjustly disadvantaging people based on skin color. Equity ensures all students have the agency to prioritize and receive "high-quality, culturally responsive academic experiences and other important youth development opportunities" (Gonzales & Vasudeva, 2021). Parity in school discipline is a way to address racism.

We need to make shifts in school discipline in order for it to be more equitable for Black, Hispanic, and special needs students and to tackle the public health issue of racism. Throughout this book, I have shared stories and research that corroborates the fact that students of color experience school discipline more harshly. Racism in a school setting can take the form of a grooming policy that discriminates against hair texture. It can also include utilizing law enforcement for non-criminal offenses as a means of discipline and classroom behavior management. By engaging in these duplicitous practices, students of color continue to be disproportionately represented in the areas of suspensions, expulsions, and even on-campus arrests. Outdated school-based policies and school environments are so deeply entrenched in various forms of racism that the ill practices over time have been normalized.

Discriminatory practices, whether intentional or not, have manifested as a colossal achievement gap between Black and Hispanic students in comparison to their White peers. For example, in a longitudinal study of high school students, researchers investigated the likelihood of students dropping out of school. The research compared school characteristics like fairness in discipline (Kotok, et al., 2016). Their data showed that high schools with better disciplinary order and stronger school attachment for the students decreased the probability of dropping out. However, when those factors were absent, students were pushed out by school administrators or they dropped out of school on their own accord. Without examining this study, reality paints an inaccurate picture that Black and Hispanic youth are misbehaved students who simply cannot learn and do not deserve an education. Further analysis depicts the impact of school discipline and what happens when policies, systems, and the school environment are misaligned. Students of color suffer the brunt of this system failure that can have a lasting impact on their futures.

As it relates to school discipline, the current system is broken and has been for quite some time. An article written for the Petrie-Flom Center suggested that educational attainment is linked to better health outcomes like jobs with high salaries that provided access to health insurance which served as a means to afford safer housing (2020). In order for students of color to reach their full potential steps must be made to remedy the current exclusionary discipline practices. Dismantling systems of oppression and ending the school-to-prison pipeline require an infusion of empathy to achieve equity. Now is the time to offer a new equity-driven mindset on ways to approach discipline and misconduct along with distinct expectations between campus leaders, educators, and school police.

Public health issues have been tackled using a framework that collectively addresses policy, systems, and the environment. When there is a concentration on all three prongs, it can be transformative. School districts can use a similar tactic when addressing disproportionate levels of discipline across different races and ethnic groups. The public health framework has shifted structures and paradigms and makes way for a diversity of stakeholders that can manufacture change. To redesign how schools approach discipline there needs to be a combination of practices that shifts laws, dismantles broken systems, and creates more inclusive school environments. Policy, system, and environmental changes can be achieved in a multitude of ways but to approach deeply ingrained racism, equity must be at the forefront.

POLICY CHANGE

Policy change occurs by modifying laws, resolutions, regulations, budgets, or rules like the school code of conduct. Shifts in policy are pivotal to producing desired behavior change over time. For example, ten years ago, the Dallas school district suspended twenty-five thousand students from their home campus, sending those students to an alternative school. Texas Appleseed estimated this blunder cost over eleven million dollars to taxpayers within the school district. On top of that, the district allocated over twenty million dollars to operate its school's police department (Breaking Rules, Breaking Budgets: The Cost of Exclusionary Discipline in Dallas ISD, 2012). This school district was in desperate need of policy changes that focused on school discipline. Over the next several years the problems of inequitable discipline practices worsened. For example, by the 2019–2020 school year, 51 percent of Black students were suspended despite only comprising 21 percent of the student body. Hispanic students were not far behind. They encompassed 43 percent of suspensions. White students, on the other hand, made up a paucity of 2 percent of all school suspensions (McNeel, 2021).

After years of inequitable treatment toward its students, the Dallas school district revised its school discipline policies. In 2017, the district passed the Racial Equity Resolution and Policy, in response to practices that contributed to institutional and systemic racism (Dallas ISD, 2017). In that same year, the district banned suspensions for students in grades preschool through second grade. In 2020, the school district received a $200,000 grant for three years to concentrate on racial equity in academics according to the district's communication platform, The Hub. The district continued to work on incremental policy reform. It took a bold step in a new direction and subsequently ended suspensions at all grade levels for low-level misconduct. In a Dallas news article, the district's Deputy Chief of Racial Equity Sharon Quinn said, "We have eliminated the three-day suspension for level one offenses and there's also a new tool that's created so administrators get to see the number of suspensions by teachers, the infractions that students have had and also how many times each student has been suspended" (Briggs, 2020). The effort was a tremendous undertaking, but funds were needed to properly implement new mandates. The following school year, the school board approved fifty million dollars to continue to reform school discipline (Dallas ISD's Alternative to Suspensions Addresses Behavioral Issues Head on, Instead of Pushing Them Aside, 2021).

This policy change was innovative because under the new guidelines, the school used Reset Rooms to replace in-school suspensions. The Reset Rooms differed from in-school suspensions because students could de-escalate in a restorative manner and could access their schoolwork. While certified teachers did not staff the Reset Rooms, trained professionals helped students maintain learning. This way, students do not fall behind in their schoolwork. Additionally, misbehaved students could receive teletherapy services, which are vital considering many other schools did not invest in mental health supports for students (Dallas ISD's Alternative to Suspensions Addresses Behavioral Issues Head On, Instead of Pushing Them Aside, 2021). Students had access to resources like mental health clinicians and staff trained in social emotional learning (Fernandez, 2021). This helped get to the root cause of student misconduct or behaviors that were normally punishable in previous school years. The new effort aimed to equip teachers and staff on restorative justice practices and social emotional learning. Time will tell how effective this policy change is in mitigating racism in schools, but it is a step in a new direction.

SYSTEMS CHANGE: THINKING DIFFERENTLY

Shifts in exclusionary discipline practices to a restorative approach is a prime example of systems change. Systems change occurs within the rules and guiding principles of an organization. Between 2011 and 2016 a transformation occurred in the area of school discipline. California schools implemented systems change through its focus on restorative justice and social and emotional learning. Suspensions declined by 33 percent and expulsions were reduced by 40 percent statewide (California Department of Education). On a local level within that same period, Le Grand High School switched its system from exclusionary discipline to a restorative justice program. The school was small, with fewer than five hundred students located in a rural town in California. The school's former discipline practices had simply been ineffective in modifying student behavior. In one school year, fifty-one students had been suspended; about 10 percent of the school's enrollment. The year before, forty-nine had been suspended and fourteen were expelled. After implementing the restorative justice program, suspensions had drastically dropped to fifteen suspensions and only one expulsion (Stevens, 2013).

In 1993, Dr. Beverly L. Parsons (formerly Anderson), the executive director of InSites, a Colorado-based nonprofit organization that focuses on education change, developed research titled "A Framework for Understanding and Assessing Systemic Change." In her analysis, she suggested six key elements are necessary for effective change in education systems (Anderson, 1993). The original intention of Dr. Parson's framework was to help stakeholders promote critical thinking in students and shift the focus from equating academic success with standardized learning. I was intrigued by her framework and wondered if the model could apply to school discipline. I wanted to interview her to learn what inspired her research, so I reached out blindly via email. In my message, I told her about my encounter with school discipline in high school and shared my curiosity about her framework. I felt her work was a vital component of a blueprint for equitable change in education and wanted to learn more about it.

When I spoke with Dr. Parsons, she began our conversation by stating, "I think it speaks to how deeply embedded the injustices are and the rigidity of our social systems that exist." Her statement was a preface to thoughts I shared around inequity in school discipline and the impetus for writing Kids in Cuffs. In reference to the development of her framework, she said, "We were trying to find a few of the key things that were relevant at the time with those students, to say we can't just change one of these things. We have to get multiple things going and it needs to span the whole system. It needs to do things like policy change, but it also has to get people thinking differently and learning differently and understanding a paradigm shift of an old way of thinking." I believed in the efficacy of her model and wanted to draw attention to how its elements could function through the lens of school discipline.

To do that, I examined the progress of the aforementioned Le Grand High School as a case study using a news article from *ACEs Too High*. *ACEs Too High* is a news site that investigates a myriad of adverse childhood experiences as well as how organizations implement research-based policies. Before diving into the comparison, I asked Dr. Parsons if she thought her framework could address transformations in school discipline. "When you're trying to change a fundamental mindset that people don't even realize they have, they need to engage in actions along with reflection and discussion. The process of fundamental change in one's way of viewing the world is complex." I understood that to mean converting to new systems required mapping out a multifaceted strategic plan along with the proper tools. From there, I began examining the six key elements of her research.

In Dr. Parson's framework, the first principle is visioning. Visioning allows for a reimagining of what discipline could be from the perspective of multiple stakeholders. The journey to restorative justice began at Le Grand High School when campus leaders solicited the help of restorative justice consultants to educate staff about the program. After developing a vision for how school discipline could change, the school board passed a resolution in support of the new direction (Stevens, 2013). This eradicated the zero-tolerance discipline policy and replaced it with practices that better supported students.

Public and political support was the second element to build continuous buy-in for the new endeavor. This component was vital to sustaining momentum because change occurs over time. The school principal at Le Grand High

School, Javier Martinez, was quoted as saying, "We understand that it's difficult to change, especially in such a drastic form. We're asking them to drop everything they know about how to discipline students, everything their parents' generation knew about disciplining students" (Stevens, 2013). His comment admitted that Le Grand High School had engaged in impertinent discipline practices that had been passed down and normalized but the school was working to do better.

The third principle involved networking to evaluate the effectiveness of the new effort and getting rid of outdated structures. It brings along new partners with innovative ideas and opinions. At Le Grand High School, parents and community members were supportive of the effort and similar partnerships. The program was working, and data showed improvements in student behavior. In addition to the student behavior challenges, concerns about other public health issues plagued the community. The restorative justice program was implemented to redirect exclusionary discipline but was also paired with another program that focused on public health. When speaking about the expansion of the partnerships, Principal Martinez believed, "A few years ago, I would have been fired for opening our campus to the community. But this idea of granting community members access to our school to improve the health of our residents came about because obesity is one of our major concerns—44 percent of Merced County residents are obese" (Stevens, 2013).

Administrative roles and responsibilities were identified as the fourth element in Dr. Parson's systems change framework. School leaders were responsible for trickling down information and system changes. Administrators needed to support teacher development in new doctrines. As part of the restorative justice initiative Le Grand High School created the Thinkery, a room where students could calm down if their behavior was inappropriate in class (Steven, 2013). At the beginning of the school year both classroom teachers and students created a set of agreements they would adhere to while in class. If students violated the agreement, they either went to the Thinkery or had a mediation session with a conflict resolution specialist and the teacher. This entire process was different from normal practices around school discipline but worked effectively when leaders provided training.

Teaching and learning changes were the fifth element of the framework that required not just a mindset shift but research and best practices on how to transfer skills. This element may be the most important because of how educators understand system change is vital for success. After the Le Grand school district passed a restorative justice resolution it needed to be communicated as a new way to deal with discipline problems that surface. To do that, educators were separated into training cohorts where they worked with consultants on restorative frameworks for four days. During that time, substitute teachers were enlisted to teach students while the educators were in training. By doing this, students were still supported in the classroom and school administrators showed teachers this new effort was a priority for the school.

Lastly, Parson's researcher suggested that state and local policy alignment is integral for any new practice. Systems change and policy change can be done separately but are more effective when they are done in tandem. In systems change, this can include allocating funds for new curriculum, training and programs, and assessments. In support of her argument, I recognized that around the time of the systems change at Le Grand High School, the California Assembly's Education Committee also worked on policies to make schools more equitable. As a point, the assembly voted to restrict the usage of vague language by school administrators when suspending students (Bill History: HB 420, 2014). The goal was to eliminate the disproportionality of discretionary suspensions. All efforts were working together to create equity for students. The new funding appropriation seemed to embody the blueprint Dr. Parson created. Principal Martinez believed, "Over the last two years, we've changed the way that we discipline students. We're firm, but respectful of the student's feelings. We listen. We don't shout. It's taking time, but we're moving in the right direction" (Steven, 2013). His words espoused empathy that all students were worthy of.

ENVIRONMENTAL CHANGES

Environmental changes are modifications to the physical environment. The school environment is the one tangible aspect of the public health framework in that it is more salient than policy or systems change. In educational settings, removing metal detectors from schools is an example of an environmental change. Environmental changes can drastically improve the school's climate, which describes how both students and the adult staff experience school life (National School Council, 2020). School climate can influence both mental health and conditions for learning. It goes without saying that positive school environments are ideal, and small interventions that change the environment can be beneficial.

Many school buildings have metal detectors that are part of their school environment. Each day students must walk through those metal detectors as a precursor to starting their school day. The devices became prevalent in the 1980s and gradually increased through the 1990s as a supposed way to prevent violence (Schildrout & Grogan). This surge was in tandem with increases in school police budgets. According to the National School Safety and Security Services, a consulting firm on school safety, metal detectors are mostly used in "some larger urban districts with a history of chronic weapons offenses." By this definition campuses with high crime rates warrant metal detectors to uncover weapons and prevent crime and keep students safe. Yet researchers found that race and socioeconomic status are a predictor of where metal detectors are placed. As a result, Black and Hispanic students in a high-poverty neighborhood were more likely to walk through a metal detector than their more affluent White counterparts (Sparks, 2020). Though the probability of crime is not necessarily a deciding factor, race is.

Other research has suggested that metal detectors are not extremely effective in preventing violence in schools. A report by WestEd Justice and Prevention Center suggested that the reason the devices are inept is that they are often improperly operated. Resource appropriation was also a factor. Metal detectors can cost between $4,000 to $5,000 per unit as well as can be costly to maintain. Most schools do not often allocate funding toward their maintenance. Lastly, they were ineffective because staff are not always proficiently trained on how to use the equipment. Interestingly enough, no strong data suggested metal detectors kept students safe.

However, data indicates racism has been at play in schools where metal detectors are placed. For example, in 2015, 48 percent of Black students and 38 percent of Hispanic students in New York attended a school that had installed a metal detector. In comparison, only 15 percent of White students attended a school with a metal detector (Schildrout and Grogan, 2019). The WestEd Justice and Prevention Center report also revealed students felt less safe when metal detectors were present compared to students who attended schools that lacked the device. The report noted that the mere presence of a metal detector in a school, led students to perceive violence and disorder at their campus. A simple removal of the intrusive devices could be a huge step toward equity because it can alter how Black, Hispanic, and low-income students experience the school environment.

We simply need to strive for sustainable change through an equity lens. Striving for equity in education requires a multifaceted approach from many stakeholders. It's a partnership that can elevate the voices of parents, students, teachers, community partners, philanthropists, and policymakers. It is hard work, but incredibly necessary. My experience with harsh school discipline happened twenty years ago but similar practices are still ongoing. I emphatically believe no student should ever have to experience such a traumatic situation. I also believe there is a much better way to do things for posterity when there is an effort to alter policy, systems, and school environments.

CLOSE YOUR EYES AND IMAGINE

Race has long been a driver of discipline inequity in schools. There is ample research that shows students of color are inordinately impacted. Unfair disciplinary treatment starts as early as preschool and remains fairly persistent through high school. Students of color are often suspended, expelled, and/or arrested more than their White counterparts. When students experience discipline that removes them from their classrooms, they lose out on academic instructions. Districts do not have policies that require campuses to supplement missed learning opportunities for suspended students. These practices deprive students of an education, which is a social determinant of health. It not only impacts students as individuals, but it also impacts their families, communities, and society as a whole. Let's reimagine better for our youth.

An infusion of restorative justice programs in lieu of punitive discipline is a relatively simple starting point for changing systems and school environments. Many schools across the nation have adopted various versions of restorative justice programs. It's a tool to help educators manage their classrooms as well as engage students in alternative ways to address issues. The results have included reductions in both suspensions and lost instruction time. Another way to eradicate the current system is to invest in social-emotional learning and other resources that supplement mental health wellness.

There is a linkage between school discipline, academic performance, and psycho-social difficulty with punishment in school contributing to psychological problems (Cameron and Sheppard, 2006). Students need access to mental health counselors, school nurses, psychiatrists, and social workers on campus. For many students, their introduction to receiving these supports starts at school. Like all people, youth experience trauma and stress and need to learn positive ways to manage their emotions. Knowing that exclusionary discipline does not deter misbehavior, schools should rely on other interventions.

As schools innovate and focus on empathy, antiquated systems should be evaluated for effectiveness. School leaders also have an opportunity to reassess the definition of "safety" and the role of police on campus. During the 2021–2022 school year, Detroit Public Schools experienced a shortage in security staff. Their school security officers were responsible for monitoring the front desk at schools and maintaining order in hallways. To address the immediate shortage, some schools hired parents to serve as greeters in the school building (Bakuli, 2021). While this solution was only temporary, it could have a positive impact on students, as it is an alternative to traditional security or police.

Meanwhile, it's time to shatter the myth that the advent of police in schools originated to counter school violence and school shootings in the 1990s. On the contrary, the relationship was created to uphold systems of segregation, which fundamentally marginalized Blacks and other students of color. While outstanding officers serve in schools, as a whole school police are strong contributors to the school-to-prison-pipeline. Incarcerating students is not the most empathic way to respond to behavior challenges in youth.

We have the power to create equity and empathy in education through advocating for changes to racially biased policies and practices. Policy change can be multilayered and take place at the federal, state, or local levels. Local policy changes can start with the school board or city council. School board or city council meetings are avenues where teachers, parents, and students can mobilize to advocate for specific agenda items or budget allocations. Stakeholders can take action by testifying at those meetings or providing written testimony on the items that are important to them. In this book, I shared examples of school districts that were successful in eliminating police in schools. Those movements were birthed at school board and/or city council meetings.

If this undertaking seems too big, another way to advocate for change is to have a conversation with the school principal or classroom teacher at your child's school. Conversations can initiate new relationships and uncover common interests. It can inspire new ideas and provide another point of view. Engaging students in the work of change is also vital because they are the ones closest to the issue and most impacted. Students can write letters, sign petitions, or raise awareness on social media platforms. By the time many of them finish high school, they will be eligible to vote, and we should foster the importance of being civically engaged early on. The possibilities to enact change are countless; however, nothing can be changed until it is faced.

On the day I finished writing this book, I created a shopping list for my son. On it were school uniforms, crayons, glue sticks, masks, and hand sanitizer. My son was overly enthusiastic because he was starting school...again. The night before, he asked me to braid his hair like his favorite rapper. He wanted to wear a new hairstyle instead of his signature curly cut. I obliged him and secretly prayed that his braids would not pose a problem in school. The next morning, we walked to class to start his first day in kindergarten at our neighborhood school.

The community was flooded with so much youthful energy! The sidewalks were filled with children and the crossing guard whistle blared as she signaled us to proceed. School staff were outside of the building welcoming students to the new academic year. For a second, I closed my eyes and imagined a school year that supported students' needs both academically and mentally. In that brief moment, I pictured students of color learning in environments teeming with empathy. Black boys were not vilified for their youthful behavior. Students with disabilities received the support they needed to thrive. Educators uplifted diversity and celebrated cultural differences. Mental health wellness was a focal point for students and staff. Everyone received what they needed in my daydream. When I opened my eyes, I knew this reality was indeed possible when we strive for equity and empathy in education.

BE THE CHANGE: TAKE ACTION

To learn more ways to take action, download a complimentary workbook at www.arsheillmonsanto.com/workbooks.

ACKNOWLEDGMENTS

——

I'd like to acknowledge the people and the stories shared within the book. I hope their words shine light on the world.

My family: Nicholas and Kingston Monsanto, The Sinclair/ Creasy family: Theresa Creasy, Chaneill Creasy, Mikesha Sinclair, Chris Borek, Michael Sinclair, and Ami Grindney. My nieces Brooklynn Lloyd, Ohanna Sinclair, Miangle Sinclar, Rythem Sinclair, Lennox Ray Borek, Shiloh Iman Borek, Mia and Jalia Ross, and my nephew Kash Sinclair.

Dr. Anita Wadhwa, Angela Cobian, Jasmin Colvin, Dr. Beverly Parsons, Chief David Kimberly and Assistant Chief Marlon Runnels, Satoria Ray, Sandra Godina, Dr. Rhoda Freelon, Andrew Hairston and the Texas Appleseed Project, Sarah Guidry and the Earl Carl Institute at Texas Southern University, Eric Koester with the Creators Institute, and New Degree Press.

I'd also like to gratefully acknowledge:

Shana Riley, Lenita, Garland, and Luke Dunlap, Chanielle Beach & Humble Wicks, Jamie Surney, Bekeela, Jeffrey and

Jason Davila, Maria Elena Fischer and PD Walks, Jordan Monsanto, Lyn-Tise Jones, Net and Anysa Monsanto, Nikki Scott, Eboni Prince, Rocaille Roberts, Tamika Hayden & Girl & Goals, Ray Fischer Sr., Barry Tyler Jr., Amber Sims, Ashley Armstrong, TC Mack, Dr. DuJuan Smith, Kris Miner, Brandon Lewis, Denise Gilmore-McPherson, Ari Randolph, Verrene and York Butler, Jasmine Quinerly, Kymberly Jamison, Jabari Stamps, Jasmine Castleberry, Willie Payton Jr., Julie Gallantry, Tatiana Jones, Kathleen Schneeman, Uyiosa Elegon, Anne Marie Parent, Damion Walker, Joshua Darden, Chris Fisher, Sheena Powenski, Wesley Garvin, Quincy Boyd and Leadership ISD, Destiny Shantell Woodbury & The Anchor School, Irene Greaves, Busola Saka, & Black Boy Thrive, Mayumi Grigsby, Brandi Bass, Bryan Reed, Candice Pettis, Brandon Williams, Lyric Flood, Trea and Taj Smith, Angel Johnson, Juliet Aniagyel, Amber and Louis Troutman, Melinda Lockhart, Maria "Gabby" Valladares, Kim Vargas, Cassandra Jones, Judy Barrett Miller, James Finck, Brent Wake, Jim Pacey, Lisa Ramirez, Rodney Martin, Andrew Wiggins, Christianna Burwell, William Yarnell, Lauren McPhail Robertson, Sheree Vodicka, Steve and Sue Fortier, Avery Lockland, and Bianca Myrtil.

Lastly, I'd like to acknowledge a few sources of inspiration:

Lorraine Hansberry, Toni Morrison, Alice Walker, Barbara Jordan, Carol Mosley Braun, Helena Stangle, Terri Broussard Williams, ONE Houston and the ONE Houston Junior Board, students from across the globe, and equity advocates fighting to make the world a much better place than the one they inherited.

BIBLIOGRAPHY

CHAPTER 1

Annie E. Casey Foundation. "When a School Calls the Police on a Student."
February 22, 2020. Video, 9:37.
https://www.youtube.com/watch?v=AYYg6RPxIMM.

Connery, Chelsea. Rep. *The Prevalence and Price of Police in Schools,* October 2020.
https://cepa.uconn.edu/wp-content/uploads/sites/399/2020/10/Issue-Brief-CEPA_C-
Connery.pdf. p.8.

Flannery, Mary Ellen. "The School-to-Prison Pipeline: Time to Shut It Down." *NEA
Today,* January 5, 2015.
http://www.nea.org/advocating-for-change/new-from-nea/school-prison-pipeline-
time-shut-it-down.

Gregory, A., & Evans, K.R. *The Starts and Stumbles of Restorative Justice in
Education: Where Do We Go from Here?* Boulder, CO: National Education Policy
Center, 2020. Accessed: September 26, 2021, from
http://nepc.colorado.edu/publication/restorative-justice.

"K-12 Education: Discipline Disparities for Black Students, Boys, and Students with
Disabilities." April 10, 2018. US GAO. US Government Accountability Office,
http://www.gao.gov/products/gao-18-258.

TEDx Talks. "School Suspensions Are an Adult Behavior | Rosemarie Allen |
TEDxMileHigh." August 1, 2016. Video, 12:23.
http://www.youtube.com/watch?v=f8nkcRMZKV4.

CHAPTER 2

Ahmed, Saeed, and Christina Walker. "There Has Been, on Average, 1 School
Shooting Every Week This Year." *CNN.* May 25, 2018.
http://www.cnn.com/2018/03/02/us/school-shootings-2018-list-trnd/index.html.

Berkshire, Jennifer, and Jack Schneider. "#91 Arrested Development: How Police Ended up in Schools." June 18, 2020. *Have You Heard?* Podcast, SoundCloud. http://soundcloud.com/haveyouheardpodcast/cops-in-schools.

Chiariello, Emily, Lisa Ann Williamson, and Walt Wolfram. "The School-to-Prison Pipeline." *Learning for Justice*, Spring 2013. https://www.learningforjustice.org/magazine/spring-2013/the-school-to-prison-pipeline.

Connery, Chelsea. Rep. *The Prevalence and Price of Police in Schools.* Center for Education Policy Analysis, October 2020. https://cepa.uconn.edu/wp-content/uploads/sites/399/2020/10/Issue-Brief-CEPA_C-Connery.pdf.

Contreras, Rebecca. *East Los Angeles Students Walkout for Educational Reform (East L.A. Blowouts), 1968.* Swarthmore, PA: Global Nonviolent Action Database, April 24, 2011. https://nvdatabase.swarthmore.edu/content/east-los-angeles-students-walkout-educational-reform-east-la-blowouts-1968.

"Counselors Not Cops: Research Behind the Call for Police-Free Schools." Chicago Teachers Union. Chicago Teachers Union Research Department, July 15, 2020. https://www.ctulocal1.org/reports/counselors-not-cops-research-behind-the-call-for-police-free-schools/.

Cox, John Woodrow, and Steven Rich. "The Extraordinary Number of Kids Who Have Endured School Shootings since Columbine." *The Washington Post.* March 25, 2018. http://www.washingtonpost.com/graphics/2018/local/us-school-shootings-history/?itid=lk_inline_manual_47.

D'Onofrio, Jessica, Craig Wall, and Cate Cauguiran. "Board Votes to Keep $33m CPS Contract with Chicago Police; Chicago Teachers Union Holds Protest March, Rally." *ABC7 Chicago. WLS-TV,* June 25, 2020. https://abc7chicago.com/cps-police-chicago-in-schools-protest/6263891/.

James, Nathan, and Gail McCallion. *School Resource Officers: Law Enforcement Officers in Schools.* Washington DC: Congressional Research Service, June 26, 2013. https://sgp.fas.org/crs/misc/R43126.pdf.

Kunichoff, Yana. "Where the Pipeline Begins: A History of Police in Chicago Public Schools." *South Side Weekly,* October 31, 2017. http://southsideweekly.com/where-the-pipeline-begins-history-police-chicago-public-schools-cps/.

"Law Enforcement Assistance Act of 1965 -- Hearings before a Subcommittee of the Senate Committee on the Judiciary, 89th Congress, 1st Session, 1965." Law Enforcement Assistance Act of 1965 -- Hearings Before a Subcommittee of the Senate Committee on the Judiciary, 89th Congress, 1st Session, 1965 | Office of Justice Programs, 1955. https://www.ojp.gov/ncjrs/virtual-library/abstracts/law-enforcement-assistance-act-1965-hearings-subcommittee-senate#additional-details-0.

Possely, Maurice. "Lee Arthur Hester." National Registry of Exonerations, September 21, 2020. http://www.law.umich.edu/special/exoneration/Pages/casedetail.aspx?caseid=5586.

Samuels, Christina A. "Where's the Threat? School Resource Officers' Views Differ Based on District Racial Makeup." *Education Week.* November 19, 2020. http://www.edweek.org/leadership/wheres-the-threat-school-resource-officers-views-differ-based-on-district-racial-makeup/2020/06.

"Texas School Safety Center." A Brief History of School-Based Law Enforcement | Texas School Safety Center. February 2016. https://txssc.txstate.edu/topics/law-enforcement/articles/brief-history.

The Origins of the School to Prison Pipeline. Advancement Project. 2016. https://americadividedseries.com/wp-content/uploads/2016/08/Divided-One-Pager-PDF.pdf.

Washington, Kendrick, and Tori Hazelton. "School Resource Officers: When the Cure Is Worse than the Disease." ACLU of Washington, June 15, 2021. https://www.aclu-wa.org/story/school-resource-officers-when-cure-worse-disease#_ftn3.

"What Was Brown v. Board of Education?" NAACP Legal Defense and Educational Fund, July 31, 2020. https://www.naacpldf.org/case-issue/landmark-brown-v-board-education/.

Zhang, Alexander. "Minneapolis Decided to Remove Police from Schools after Decades of Criticism." *Slate Magazine,* June 4, 2020. https://slate.com/news-and-politics/2020/06/minneapolis-remove-police-from-schools-history.html.

CHAPTER 3

"5 Things Educators Can Do to Address Bias in Their School." NEA EdJustice, October 11, 2019. https://neaedjustice.org/2019/10/11/5-things-educators-can-do-to-address-bias-in-their-school/.

Amico, Beverly. "Teaching Empathy: Essential for Students, Crucial for Humanity." Home - Association of Waldorf Schools of North America, October 14, 2020. https://www.waldorfeducation.org/news-resources/essentials-in-education-blog/detail/~board/essentials-in-ed-board/post/teaching-empathy-essential-for-students-crucial-for-humanity.

Barrett, Nathan, Andrew McEachin, Johnathan N. Mills, and Jon Vallant. *What Are the Sources of School Discipline Disparities by Student Race and Family Income.* New Orleans, Louisiana: Education Research Alliance for New Orleans, 2017. https://educationresearchalliancenola.org/files/publications/111417-Barrett-McEachin-Mills-Valant-What-Are-the-Sources-of-School-Discipline-Disparities-by-Student-Race-and-Family-Income.pdf.

Barth, Patte. Rep. *Educational Equity: What Does It Mean? How Do We Know When We Reach It?* Center for Public Education, January 2016. https://www.nsba.org/-/media/NSBA/File/cpe-educational-equity-research-brief-january-2016.pdf.

Burke, Minyvonne. "Boy, 9, Suspended after Teacher Sees BB Gun in His Room during Virtual Class; Family Sues." *NBCNews.com.* October 6, 2020. https://www.nbcnews.com/news/us-news/boy-9-suspended-after-teacher-sees-bb-gun-his-room-n1242275.

Canady, Maurice, Bernard James, Dr. Janet Nease. *"To Protect and Educate: The SRO & Prevention of Violence in Schools."* Hoover, AL: National Association of School Resource Officers, 2012. tasro.org/resources/Documents/NASRO-To-Protect-and-Educate-nosecurity.pdf.

Crespo, Gisela. "4th Grader Suspended for Having a BB Gun in His Bedroom During Virtual Learning." *CNN.* October 4, 2020. http://www.cnn.com/2020/09/26/us/student-suspended-gun-virtual/index.html.

Edward Monds, Kathaleena. "Black Children Continue to Be Pushed out of American Schools During Pandemic." *EdChoice,* October 9, 2020. http://www.edchoice.org/engage/black-children-continue-to-be-pushed-out-of-american-schools-during-pandemic/.

Goff, P. A., Jackson, M. C., Di Leone, B. A. L., Culotta, C. M., & DiTomasso, N. A. The Essence of Innocence: Consequences of Dehumanizing Black Children. *Journal of Personality and Social Psychology, 106*(4), 526–545. 2014. https://doi.org/10.1037/a0035663.

Loewy, Adam. "TASER Debate Continues After Settlement in Noe Niño de Rivera Case." *Loewy Law Firm Blog,* October 10, 2014. https://personalinjurylawyersaustintx.com/blog/taser-debate-continues-settlement-noe-nino-de-rivera-case/.

McLaughlin, Eliott C. "Texas Student Tased by Police Exits Coma, Enters Rehabilitation, Attorney Says." *CNN.* February 4, 2014. http://www.cnn.com/2014/01/31/us/texas-taser-high-school-student-coma.

"Mendez v. Westminster Re-Enactment." 1946. United States Courts. Retrieved: August 28, 2021. http://www.uscourts.gov/educational-resources/educational-activities/background-mendez-v-westminster-re-enactment.

Odoms, Alanah. "ACLU of Louisiana Condemns Suspension of 4th Grader Ka'mauri Harrison for BB Gun." ACLU of Louisiana, September 28, 2020. http://www.laaclu.org/en/press-releases/aclu-louisiana-condemns-suspension-4th-grader-kamauri-harrison-bb-gun.

O'Rourke, Ciara. "TASED Student 'Totally Dependent on Me,' Bastrop Mother Says." *Austin American-Statesman,* September 25, 2018. https://www.statesman.com/article/20140130/NEWS/301309710.

Peiser, Jaclyn. "A Black Seventh-Grader Played with a Toy Gun during a Virtual Class. His School Called the Police." *The Washington Post.* September 8, 2020. http://www.washingtonpost.com/nation/2020/09/08/black-student-suspended-police-toy-gun/.

"Policy Areas." In School Suspension Program Requirements: Issue Brief from the Budget Board Staff. Legislative Budget Board, Austin, TX: February 2013. http://www.lbb.state.tx.us./.

"Preventing Suspensions and Expulsions in Early Childhood Settings a Program Leader's Guide to Supporting All Children's Success." Preventing Suspensions and Expulsions in Early Childhood Settings. Accessed: September 28, 2021. https://preventexpulsion.org/1g-provide-professional-development-and-ongoing-support-for-all-program-staff-on-culturally-responsive-practices-and-implicit-bias/.

Riddle, Travis, and Stacey Sinclair. "Racial Disparities in School-Based Disciplinary Actions Are Associated with County-Level Rates of Racial Bias." PNAS. National Academy of Sciences, April 23, 2019. http://www.pnas.org/content/116/17/8255.

Roberts, Faimon A. "Tempers Flare in Six-Hour Jefferson School Board Hearing for Ka'mauri Harrison." NOLA.com, December 5, 2020. http://www.nola.com/news/education/article_6fc8d660-3681-11eb-af9d-0b6be993cb95.html.

Romero, Troy. HB83, Louisiana State Legislature, Baton Rouge, LA. November 2020. legis.la.gov/legis/BillInfo.aspx?i=239591.

Texas School Discipline Lab. School Police. Austin, TX: 2016. http://www.texasdisciplinelab.org/about/school-police/.

"The School Counselor and Discipline." The School Counselor and Discipline - American School Counselor Association (ASCA), 2019. https://schoolcounselor.org/Standards-Positions/Position-Statements/ASCA-Position-Statements/The-School-Counselor-and-Discipline.

CHAPTER 4

"Anti-Racism Policy." Albemarle County School District, 2019. https://www.k12albemarle.org/our-division/anti-racism-policy.

"Barbers Hill ISD Student Handbook: 2019-2020 School Year." Barbers Hill Independent School District, 2019. resources.finalsite.net/images/v1578332756/bhisd/gbxcdmj8opcqktcuk8sv/BHISDStudentHandbook2019-2020rev1-6-2020.pdf.

"Barbers Hill ISD Upholds Hair Policy That Led to DeAndre Arnold and Cousin's Suspensions." ABC13 Houston, KTRK-TV, July 21, 2020, abc13.com/deandre-arnold-dreadlocks-barbers-hill-high-school-hair/6325513/.

Bowers, Rhetta. "Texas HB392: 2021-2022: 87th Legislature." Austin, TX: LegiScan, 2021, legiscan.com/TX/bill/HB392/2021.

Brodsky, Alexandra. "DRESS CODED: Black Girls, Bodies, and Bias in DC Schools." National Women's Law Center, July 21, 2020. nwlc.org/resources/dresscoded/.

Carpenter, Jacob. "Wheatley Failure Puts HISD on Path to Takeover despite Strong Overall Showing on State Ratings." Houston Chronicle. August 16, 2019. www.houstonchronicle.com/news/houston-texas/houston/article/Wheatley-failure-puts-HISD-on-path-to-takeover-14308497.php.

Codes of Conduct Policies. Codes of Conduct Policies | Student Engagement Project | Nebraska. (n.d.). Accessed: September 21, 2021. https://k12engagement.unl.edu/codes-of-conduct-policies.

Cameron, M., & Sheppard, S. M. School Discipline and Social Work Practice: Application of Research and Theory to Intervention. *Oxford University Press Academic,* January 1, 2006. Accessed: September 22, 2021, from https://academic.oup.com/cs/article-abstract/28/1/15/423710?redirectedFrom=fulltext.

Craven, Morgan, Dr. Ellen Stone, and Deborah Fowler. Guarding Our Most Precious Resources: Comparing the Staffing of Counselors and Mental Health Professionals to Police in Texas Schools. Austin, TX: Texas Appleseed, March 25, 2019. www.texasappleseed.org/sites/default/files/Guarding%20our%20most%20 precious%20resources.pdf.

Dellinger, Hannah. "Barbers Hill ISD at Center of Another Controversy Involving Students' Hair." *Houston Chronicle,* August 25, 2021. https://www.houstonchronicle.com/news/houston-texas/education/article/barbers-hill-hair-lawsuit-policy-suspensions-16410999.php?cmpid=gsa-chron-result.

Devos, Betsy and Kenneth Marcus. *2015-2016 Civil Rights Data Collection School Climate and Safety Report.* Washington, DC: US Department of Education, Office of Civil Rights, 2018. https://www2.ed.gov/about/offices/list/ocr/docs/school-climate-and-safety.pdf.

"Ensuring Safe and Supportive School Climates in Texas." *The Education Trust,* November 30, 2020. edtrust.org/resource/ensuring-safe-and-supportive-school-climates-in-texas/.

Epstein, Rebecca, Jamilia Blake, and Thalia Gonzalez, Rep. *Girlhood Interrupted: The Erasure of Black Girls' Childhood,* 2017. https://genderjusticeandopportunity.georgetown.edu/wp-content/uploads/2020/06/ girlhood-interrupted.pdf.

Fisher, Ian. "Kelly Bans Choke Holds by Officers. *The New York Times,* November 24, 1993. http://www.nytimes.com/1993/11/24/nyregion/kelly-bans-choke-holds-by-officers.html.

Gowdy, ShaCamree. "Texas School Board Will Not Be Changing Policy That Led to Suspension of Two Black Male Students with Dreadlocks." *Houston Chronicle,* July 24, 2020. www.houstonchronicle.com/news/education/article/Texas-School-Board-votes-unanimously-to-uphold-15432076.php.

Grieder, Erica. "Grieder: Suspension of Barbers Hill ISD Student over Dreadlocks Puts Focus on Hair Discrimination." *Houston Chronicle,* Feb. 12, 2020. www.houstonchronicle.com/news/columnists/grieder/article/suspension-student-hair-love-Oscars-Deandre-Arnold-15048886.php.

Henderson, H., & Bourgeois, J. W. *Penalizing black hair in the name of academic success is undeniably racist, unfounded, and against the law.* Brookings. February 23, 2021. https://www.brookings.edu/blog/how-we-rise/2021/02/23/penalizing-black-hair-in-the-name-of-academic-success-is-undeniably-racist-unfounded-and-against-the-law/.

Jones, Britney. "Reducing Racism in Schools: The Promise of Anti-Racist Policies." Neag School of Education. University of Connecticut, September 22, 2020. https://education.uconn.edu/2020/09/22/reducing-racism-in-schools-the-promise-of-anti-racist-policies/#.

Justin, Raga. "Texas School District's Dreadlocks Ban Discriminatory, Federal Court Rules." *The Texas Tribune*, August 19, 2020. www.texastribune.org/2020/08/18/texas-school-dreadlocks-ban/.

King, John B. and Catherine Lhamon "*2013-2014 Civil Rights Data Collection: A First Look.*" Washington, DC: United States Department of Education, Office of Civil Rights, June 7, 2015. www2.ed.gov/about/offices/list/ocr/docs/2013-14-first-look.pdf.

Knott, Katherine. "Report Evaluates Implementation so Far of Albemarle Schools' Anti-Racism Policy." *The Daily Progress*, November 15, 2020. https://dailyprogress.com/news/local/education/report-evaluates-implementation-so-far-of-albemarle-schools-anti-racism-policy/article_0534eb7a-26d4-11eb-a15d-c35cce8d9b52.html.

Knott, Katherine. "Students Seek Lasting Change with Albemarle Anti-Racism Policy." *The Daily Progress*, December 15, 2018, https://dailyprogress.com/news/local/students-seek-lasting-change-with-albemarle-anti-racism-policy/article_0aa5fdc4-00c0-11e9-8d35-cf82d77a63ed.html.

"LDF Files Public Records Request on Behalf of De'andre Arnold and Family." NAACP Legal Defense and Educational Fund, February 5, 2020. http://www.naacpldf.org/press-release/ldf-represents-mr-deandre-arnold-and-family-files-public-records-request/.

Lohr, David. "School Resource Officers Accused of Using Excessive Force (Video)." *HuffPost*. December 7, 2017. http://www.huffpost.com/entry/ixel-perez-student-tackled_n_5766324.

Morris, Edward W, and Brea L. Perry. "Girls Behaving Badly? Race, Gender, and Subjective Evaluation in the Discipline of African American Girls - Edward W. Morris, Brea L. Perry, 2017." *SAGE Journals*, February 1, 2017. https://journals.sagepub.com/doi/10.1177/0038040717694876.

"Policy Evaluation Report." Albemarle County School District, 2020. https://www.k12albemarle.org/our-division/anti-racism-policy/policy-evaluation-report.

Riddle, T., & Sinclair, S. *Racial Disparities in School-based Disciplinary Actions Are Associated with County-level Rates of Racial Bias.* PNAS. April 23, 2019. https://www.pnas.org/content/116/17/825.

"Student Requirements / Code of Conduct." Code of Conduct. Houston Independent School District. Accessed: September 6, 2021. https://www.houstonisd.org/codeofconduct.

Texas School Discipline Lab. *School Police.* Austin, TX: 2016. http://www.texasdisciplinelab.org/about/school-police/.

"The CROWN Research Study." *https://www.thecrownact.com/Resources,*
The Joy Collective, 2019, www.thecrownact.com/resources.

CHAPTER 5

"About NASRO." Hoover, AL: National Association of School Resource Officers, 2021.
https://www.nasro.org/faq/#:~:text=The%20National%20Association%20of%20
School,SROs%20that%20NASRO%20has%20trained.

Brown, Lee. "Bodycam Video Shows Teen Struggling for Gun before Being Shot by
Cops." *New York Post,* April 22, 2021.
nypost.com/2021/04/22/video-shows-teen-struggling-for-gun-before-being-shot-by-cops/.

Dilliberti, Melissa, Michael Jackson, Samuel Correa, and Zoe Padgett. *Crime,
Violence, Discipline and Safety in US Public Schools: Findings from the School Survey
on Climate and Safety: 2017-18.* Washington, DC: National Center for Education
Statistics, United States Department of Education, July 2019.
nces.ed.gov/pubs2019/2019061.pdf.

Hairston, Andrew, Dr. Vicki Luna Sullivan, and Dr. Ellen Stone. *Education
Transformed: The K-12 Experience in Texas During the Coronavirus Pandemic.*
Austin, Texas: Texas Appleseed, Mar. 31, 2021. p.29.
www.texasappleseed.org/sites/default/files/EducationTransformed_Report032921-Fin.pdf.

"History." *Klein ISD, Promise2Purpose,* 2021,
kleinisd.net/district/police/history.

Murphy, Ryan, and Annie Daniel. Klein ISD: Texas Public Schools, *Texas Tribune.*
April 5, 2019.
schools.texastribune.org/districts/klein-isd/.

Rojas, Rick. "One High School, Five Students Fatally Shot." *The New York Times,*
April 23, 2021.
www.nytimes.com/2021/04/23/us/knoxville-anthony-thompson.html.

Rudd, T. *Racial Disproportionality in School Discipline: Implicit Bias is Heavily
Implicated* (pp. 2–8). Columbus, OH: Kirwan Institute for the Study of Race and
Ethnicity, 2014.

Student Code of Conduct: 2020-2021." *Klein ISD Promise2Purpose,* 2020.
www.vision.kleinisd.net.

Texas State Legislature. House Bill 2684. Austin, Texas: May 29, 2015.
https://capitol.texas.gov/tlodocs/84R/billtext/pdf/HB02684F.pdf.

CHAPTER 6

Allen, Terry, Bryan, Isaac, Guerero, Andrew, Teng, Alvin, and Lytle-Hernandez,
Kelly. *Policing Our Students: An Analysis of LA School Police Department Data (2014-
2017).* Los Angeles, CA: The Million Dollar Hoods Project, 2018.
http://milliondollarhoods.org/wp-content/uploads/2018/10/Policing-Our-Students-
MDH-Report-Final.pdf.

"Board of Education of the City of Los Angeles." Governing Board of the Los Angeles Unified School District, February 16, 2021. laschoolboard.org/sites/default/files/02-16-21SpclBdOBWithMaterialsColor.pdf

French-Marcelin, Megan and Sarah Hinger. *Bullies in Blue: Origins and Consequences of School Policing.* New York, New York: American Civil Liberties Union Foundation, April 12, 2017. https://www.aclu.org/report/bullies-blue-origins-and-consequences-school-policing.

Ceasar, Stephen. "LA Schools Police Will Return Grenade Launchers but Keep Rifles, Armored Vehicle." *Los Angeles Times,* September 17, 2014. www.latimes.com/local/lanow/la-me-schools-weapons-20140917-story.html.

"Data Tables (XLSX)." US Bureau of Labor Statistics, August 10, 2021. https://www.bls.gov/cps/effects-of-the-coronavirus-covid-19-pandemic.htm.

Faircloth, Ryan. "Minneapolis Public Schools Terminates Contract with Police Department over George Floyd's Death." *Star Tribune,* June 3, 2020. www.startribune.com/mpls-school-board-ends-contract-with-police-for-school-resource-officers/570967942/?refresh=true.

Harris, Kara. "There's a Movement to Defund School Police, Too." *Bloomberg.com,* August 24, 2020. https://www.bloomberg.com/news/articles/2020-08-24/minneapolis-denver-and-oakland-defund-school-police.

"Home." *La Educación Es Liberación // Education Is Liberation,* 2021. padresunidos.org/?v=402f03a963ba.

Kohli, Sonali. "Eliminate School Police, LA Teachers Union Leaders Say." *Los Angeles Times,* June 9, 2020. www.latimes.com/california/story/2020-06-08/defund-school-police-utla-blm.

Kholi, Solani and Howard Blume. "For Teen Activists, Defunding School Police Has Been a Decade in the Making." *Los Angeles Times,* June 15, 2020. www.latimes.com/california/story/2020-06-15/defund-police-schools-case-security-guards-campus.

King, John B. and Catherine Lhamon "*2013-2014 Civil Rights Data Collection: A First Look.*" Washington, DC: United States Department of Education, Office of Civil Rights, June 7, 2015. www2.ed.gov/about/offices/list/ocr/docs/2013-14-first-look.pdf.

Kunichoff, Yana. "Where the Pipeline Begins: A History of Police in Chicago Public Schools." *South Side Weekly,* October 31, 2017. southsideweekly.com/where-the-pipeline-begins-history-police-chicago-public-schools-cps/.

"LA School Police / Los Angeles School Police Department." *Los Angeles Unified School District / Homepage,* achieve.lausd.net/laspd. 2019. Accessed: 19, April 2021.

Lathan, Grenita. "060120_Floyd Statement." Houston Independent School District, June 1, 2020.
https://www.houstonisd.org/cms/lib2/TX01001591/Centricity/Domain/4/060120_Floyd_statement.pdf.

"Office of Gun Violence Prevention." Office Of Gun Violence Prevention | Colorado General Assembly, June 1, 2021.
https://leg.colorado.gov/bills/hb21-1299.

Riski, Tess. "Mayor Ted Wheeler Removes Portland Police Officers From All Public Schools, Effective Immediately." *Willamette Week*, May 31, 2020.
www.wweek.com/news/schools/2020/06/04/mayor-ted-wheeler-removes-portland-police-officers-from-all-public-schools-effective-immediately.

"School Based Mental Health." School Based Mental Health | Youth.gov. Accessed: October 6, 2021.
https://youth.gov/youth-topics/youth-mental-health/school-based#_ftn.

Shuttleworth, Margaret. "LA School Board Removes Officers from Campuses, Approves Black Student Investment." *FOX 11 Los Angeles*, February 17, 2021.
www.foxla.com/news/la-school-board-removes-officers-from-campuses-approves-black-student-investment?fbclid=IwAR0XGwzIpybELITST5vE2SQcW3bdqFUxuDtWKtDccMeAzjpLuTnLQiDIUaE.

"Supporting Mental Health In Schools." American Academy of Pediatrics.National Center for School Mental Health, March 2021.
https://downloads.aap.org/dochw/dshp/Supporting_Mental_Health_in_Schools_Final_Report-June_2021.pdf.

Quinton, Sophie. "Denver School Board Votes to Remove Police From Schools." *The Pew Charitable Trusts*, June 12, 2020. www.pewtrusts.org/en/research-and-analysis/blogs/stateline/2020/06/12/denver-school-board-votes-to-remove-police-from-schools.

Whitney, Daniel G, and Mark D Peterson. "US National and State-Level Prevalence of Mental Health Disorders and Disparities of Mental Health Care Use in Children." *Journal of American Medical Association*, April 1, 2019.
https://www.ncbi.nlm.nih.gov/pmc/articles/PMC6450272/.

CHAPTER 7

Alameda County Restorative Juvenile Justice Strategic Plan. Oakland, CA: Oakland Unified School District, December 2012.
https://www.ousd.org/cms/lib/CA01001176/Centricity/Domain/97/RJ_Strategic_Plan_4_8_09.pdf.

Allensworth, Elaine, Nick Mader, Shannon Guiltinan, Lauren Sartain, Rachel Levenstein, W. David Stevens, Michelle Hanh Huynh, Shanette Porter. *Discipline Practices in Chicago Schools*. Chicago, IL: UChicago Consortium on School Research, March 2015.
consortium.uchicago.edu/publications/discipline-practices-chicago-schools-trends-use-suspensions-and-arrests.

California Legislative Information. "AB-1729 Pupil Rights: Suspension or Expulsion: Alternatives and Other Means of Correction." 2012. leginfo.legislature.ca.gov/faces/billNavClient.xhtml?bill_id=201120120AB1729

Frey, Susan. "Oakland Ends Suspensions for Willful Defiance, Funds Restorative Justice." *EdSource*, May 26, 2015. edsource.org/2015/oakland-ends-suspensions-for-willful-defiance-funds-restorative-justice/79731.

Fronius, Trevor, Sean Darling-Hammond, Hannah Persson, Sarah Gukenburg, Nancy Hurley, Anthony Petrosino. "Restorative Justice in US Schools." *Justice and Prevention Research Center*, March 2019. www.wested.org/wp-content/uploads/2019/04/resource-restorative-justice-in-u-s-schools-an-updated-research-review.pdf.

Gutierrez, Rhona Rae, and Pauline Lipman. August 2012. *Dyett High School & the Three D's of Chicago School Reform: Destabilization, Disenfranchisement, Disinvestment.* Chicago, IL: Collaborative for Equity and Justice in Education, University of Chicago College of Education, ceje.uic.edu/wp-content/uploads/2013/11/Fact-Sheet-Dyett1.pdf.

Perez, Juan. "Teachers Complain about Revised CPS Discipline Policy." *Chicago Tribune*, August 18, 2019. www.chicagotribune.com/news/ct-cps-discipline-concerns-met-20150225-story.html.

Reilly, Katie. "Oakland Ends School Police Force After Years of Activism." *Time*, June 25, 2020. time.com/5859452/oakland-school-police/.

Restorative Justice for Oakland Youth (RJOY). "Our History." Last modified in 2021, https://rjoyoakland.org.

"Resolution of the Board of Education Oakland Unified School District." Oakland Unified School District, December 16, 2009. www.ousd.org/cms/lib/CA01001176/Centricity/Domain/97/Board_Resolution_RJ_final.pdf.

Tepperman, Jean. "A People-Focused Solution." *East Bay Express*, May 23, 2013, eastbayexpress.com/a-people-focused-solution-1/.

US Department of Education. "US Department of Education Announces Voluntary Resolution of Oakland Unified School District Civil Rights Investigation." US Department of Education press release, September 28, 2012. www.ed.gov/news/press-releases/us-department-education-announces-voluntary-resolution-oakland-unified-school-district-civil-rights-investigation.

Zehr Institute."Restorative Justice? What's That?" Last modified in 2021. zehr-institute.org/what-is-rj/.

CHAPTER 8

"Achieving Excellence & Equity Through Resource Use: ERS Summary Report for Dallas ISD." The Hub Dallas ISD, Dallas Independent School District, 2020. thehub.dallasisd.org/newsroom/wp-content/uploads/2020/07/FinalDallas-ISD-ERS-Final-Report-06092020.pdf.

Anderson, Beverly. "A Framework for Understanding and Assessing Systems Change." ERIC Institute of Education Sciences, Education Commission of the States, February 1993. files.eric.ed.gov/fulltext/ED375459.pdf.

Bakuli, Ethan. "Security Guard Shortage Drives Detroit Schools to Raise Pay and Prompts Safety Concerns." Chalkbeat Detroit. Chalkbeat Detroit, September 16, 2021. https://detroit.chalkbeat.org/2021/9/16/22678430/security-guard-shortage-detroit-schools-raise-pay-safety-concerns.

"Bill History: HB 420." Bill History, September 27, 2014. leginfo.legislature.ca.gov/faces/billHistoryClient.xhtml?bill_id=201320140AB420.

Briggs, Shakira. DISD Touts Plan to Promote Racial Equity Across District. *Spectrum News.* November 16, 2020. spectrumlocalnews.com/tx/south-texas-el-paso/education/2020/11/16/d-i-s-d--touts-plan-to-promote-racial-equity--opportunities-for-black-students.

"Breaking Rules, Breaking Budgets: The Cost of Exclusionary Discipline in Dallas ISD." Texas Appleseed, March 27, 2012. www.texasappleseed.org/breaking-rules-breaking-budgets-cost-exclusionary-discipline-dallas-isd.

California Department of Education. State Schools Chief Tom Torlakson Announces Decline in Suspensions and Expulsions for Third Year in a Row. http://www.cde.ca.gov/nr/ne/yr16/yr16rel5.asp.

Cameron, Mark, and Sandra M. Sheppard. "School Discipline and Social Work Practice: Application of Research and Theory to Intervention." *Oxford University Press Academic,* January 1, 2006. https://academic.oup.com/cs/article-abstract/28/1/15/423710?redirectedFrom=fulltext.

"Dallas Education Foundation Receives $200,000 Grant from USAA to Advance Racial Equality." The Hub, December 18, 2020. thehub.dallasisd.org/2020/12/18/dallas-education-foundation-receives-200000-grant-from-usaa-to-advance-racial-equality/.

"Dallas ISD's Alternative to Suspensions Addresses Behavioral Issues Head on, Instead of Pushing Them Aside." The Hub, September 9, 2021. https://thehub.dallasisd.org/2021/09/09/dallas-isds-alternative-to-suspensions-addresses-behavioral-issues-head-on-instead-of-pushing-them-aside/.

Fernandez, Demond. "Dallas ISD Will No Longer Suspend High School and Middle School Students, Introduces 'Reset Centers' as New Disciplinary Action." *wfaa.com,* September 23, 2021. https://www.wfaa.com/article/news/education/dallas-isd-will-no-longer-use-suspensions-for-high-school-middle-school-students-introduces-reset-centers/287-4e81934e-3b99-4ca0-aada-b4f663e5a302.

Gonzalez, T., A. Etow, & C. De La Vega. *School Discipline is a Public Health Crisis.*
Cambridge, MA: Petrie-Flom Center, October 5, 2020.
https://blog.petrieflom.law.harvard.edu/2020/10/06/school-discipline-is-a-public-
health-crisis/.

Gonzales, D. & A. Vasudeva. *Looking Back to Accelerate Forward: Toward a Policy
Paradigm that Advances Equity and Improvement.* Washington, DC: The Aspen
Institute Education & Society Program, April 14, 2021.
https://www.aspeninstitute.org/publications/looking-back-to-accelerate-forward/

Kotok, Stephen, Sakiko Ikoma and Katerina Bodovski. *School Climate and Dropping
Out of School in the Era of Accountability.* Chicago, IL: American Journal of
Education, University of Chicago Press, July 31, 2016.
eric.ed.gov/?q=school%2Bclimate%2Band%2Bdrop%2Bout&id=EJ1108826

McNeel, Bekah. "Reinventing School Discipline in Texas: After Years of Unequal
Punishment for Black Students, Dallas ISD Moves Toward Historic End to Most
Suspensions." *The 74 Million,* April 27, 2021.
www.the74million.org/article/dallas-proposes-rewrite-to-disciplinary-code-that-
fell-heavily-on-black-students-end-to-many-suspensions/.

"Parents and Students Invited to Effective Discipline Feedback Session." *The Hub,*
May 13, 2021.
thehub.dallasisd.org/2021/05/12/parents-and-students-invited-to-effective-
discipline-feedback-session/.

"Racism and Health." Centers for Disease Control and Prevention, Office of Minority
Health and Health Equity, April 12, 2021.
www.cdc.gov/healthequity/racism-disparities/index.html.

Schildrout, J., & Grogan, K. "Are Metal Detectors Effective at Making Schools Safer?"
San. Francisco, CA: WestEd. 2019.
https://www.wested.org/resources/are-metal-detectors-effective-at-making-schools-safer.

Sparks, Sarah D. "Study Finds Metal Detectors More Common in High-Minority
Schools." *Education Week,* December 1, 2020.
www.edweek.org/leadership/study-finds-metal-detectors-more-common-in-high-
minority-schools/2011/08.

Stevens, Jane Ellen. "The Restorative Justice League of Le Grand High School Jumps
in to Save the Day." *ACEs Too High,* California Endowment, October 2, 2013.
www.acestoohigh.com/2013/09/30/the-restorative-justice-league-of-le-grand-high-school.